Practical School Security

Basic Guidelines for Safe and Secure Schools

Kenneth S. Trump

CORWIN PRESS, INC.
A Sage Publications Company
Thousand Oaks, California

For information:

Corwin Press Inc.
A Sage Publications Company
2455 Teller Road
Thousand Oaks, California 91320
E-mail: order@corwin.sagepub.com

SAGE Publications Ltd.
6 Bonhill Street
London EC2A 4PU
United Kingdom

SAGE Publications India Pvt. Ltd.
M-32 Market
Greater Kailash I
New Delhi 110 048 India

Printed in the United States of America

Library of Congress Cataloging-in-Publication Data

Trump, Kenneth S.
    Practical school security: Basic guidelines for safe and secure
schools / by Kenneth S. Trump.
        p.   cm.
    Includes bibliographical references.
    ISBN 0-8039-6353-X (cloth : acid-free paper).—ISBN 0-8039-6354-8
(pbk. : acid-free paper)
        1. Schools—Security measures—United States—Handbooks, manuals, etc.
    2. Schools—United States—Safety measures—Handbooks, manuals, etc.
    3. School violence—United States—Handbooks, manuals, etc. I. Title.
    LB2866.T78 1997
    363.11'371—dc21   97-33725

This book is printed on acid-free paper.

98 99 00 01 02 03 10 9 8 7 6 5 4 3 2 1

Production Editor: Astrid Virding
Production Assistant: Denise Santoyo
Editorial Assistant: Kristen Gibson
Typesetter/Designer: Marion Warren
Cover Designer: Marcia M. Rosenburg
Print Buyer: Anna Chin

Contents

Foreword

In my research on gangs during the past 12 years, I have become keenly aware of the important role of the schools in the prevention and control of gang-related violence and other threats to the safety of students, faculty, and staff. Unfortunately, many school officials continue to engage in denial and often appear to be more concerned about their school's image than about the safety of the students entrusted to their care. And many other officials and teachers, genuinely searching for assistance with gang-related problems and other school safety and security issues, have not been able to identify sound, comprehensive resource materials to assist them.

This book addresses that need. It is written by a very well-respected professional who has extensive firsthand experience in dealing with school safety and security issues, including those related to gangs, violence, drugs, weapons, and strangers in our schools. I first met Ken Trump during my initial field research on gangs, and in the intervening years, I have discovered that he is very well-informed about all of these issues and is adept at helping others develop positive approaches to the prevention, intervention, and suppression of school-related violence. Indeed, he has developed a national reputation in the past decade and is in great demand as a trainer and workshop presenter throughout the country.

Whenever I need information concerning school safety and security issues, there are few people in the country to whom I know I can turn for accurate and complete answers, and Ken Trump is one of them. With the publication of this book, you will be able to benefit, as I have, from his expertise. In the pages that follow, he will help you understand the changing nature of threats to security and how to deal with them.

Should school systems buy metal detectors and surveillance cameras? Should school officials conduct random locker searches and use drug-sniffing dogs in their buildings? What can be done about the increased fighting that occurs in our schools? Are school uniforms and dress codes merely a fad, or do they offer real potential for the reduction of conflict and violence? Trump discusses these and other critical issues in a most enlightening and practical manner. He concludes with an insightful discussion of collaboration—working with students, parents, law enforcement, the community, and the media—as well as the need for appropriate legislation and funding.

I firmly believe that those readers who follow Trump's recommendations will find them to be of significant value in addressing the challenges posed by school violence and other threats. Schools have been neglected for too long in our efforts to formulate effective prevention and intervention strategies. They have enormous potential, but that potential is too often compromised by denial, concerns about image, and "school politics." It is time that we move past all of that and begin to recognize that our first responsibility is for the safety of the children, faculty, and staff in our schools. Only then can we ensure a learning environment that is free from fear and intimidation—the kind of environment that is associated with academic achievement and personal growth.

C. RONALD HUFF, Ph.D.
Director and Professor
School of Public Policy and Management
Ohio State University
Columbus, Ohio

Preface

In the United States, we have traditionally viewed schools as safe havens for our children. But in the past several decades, students, school staff, and parents alike have watched violence increasingly violate this sanctuary. Injuries to students and staff and disruptions of the educational process have become commonplace. Educators, law enforcement, and members of the overall school community have been forced to grasp quickly for solutions to both real and perceived security concerns.

Practical School Security resulted from a combination of two factors. First, there was a need for a basic resource for educators seeking practical, realistic guidance for improving school security. Second, professional colleagues and school leaders who attended, and received training in, my security workshops encouraged me to assemble my thoughts, experiences, and recommendations on school security into a usable format and a handy reference for busy educators seeking basic security information.

Few books on the market address violence and safety strategies from a school-specific perspective. Those in print generally cover school violence from a theoretical perspective or in the form of violence prevention curriculum materials for classroom use. A few publications dealing with practical security measures were written a decade or two ago, and only several are reportedly underway to address the increasingly difficult problems facing educators today and in the years ahead.

School security has not been fully recognized, nor accepted, as a separate, unique, and professional support service in most educational systems. Safe schools are often addressed from perspectives focusing on discipline, inclusion, ownership, curriculum on preventing violence, maintenance and cleanliness, and related issues. Although these issues are important components of safe school efforts, school security is a separate entity that is frequently missing from our written resources.

In addition, most educators have not been adequately prepared academically or in practice to deal with school-based crimes from a security perspective. There is a growing cry across the nation for new reference materials offering a practical framework and realistic strategies for reducing threats to school security. This book provides school security basics and straightforward answers. It challenges common misconceptions about school security threats and provides a starting point for educators to frame, implement, or revise their school security programs rationally and effectively.

Practical School Security is written primarily for elementary and secondary school principals, assistant principals, counselors, teachers, central office support staff, superintendents, and board members. College and university faculty involved in providing teacher preparation programs, administration and counseling certification, or continuing education programs for school personnel would also benefit from using this book in their classes. It also serves as an introductory resource for law enforcement officials who work with schools, school resource officers, school security directors and specialists, and professional associations or unions representing educational personnel. This book will also be of interest to parents, media representatives, and members of the broader school community involved in framing school security issues and identifying realistic steps for enhancing school security.

The book answers many common questions about security policies, procedures and practices. It also provides the key questions that need to be asked and answered by school leaders when assessing and resolving their security problems. This is particularly important because of the potential distortion that often occurs in dealing with the highly emotional and political nature of school security issues.

Chapters 1 through 3 establish a framework for dealing with the myths and realities of school violence that usually cloud effective handling of security issues. The real threats to school security and the impact of politics on responding to and preventing these threats are candidly discussed in the first two chapters. Chapter 3 offers practical recommendations for dealing with the threats and the politics. Collectively, these chapters set the groundwork for implementing the recommendations in the rest of the book.

Whereas Chapters 1 through 3 explain how to frame school security issues, Chapters 4 through 7 explain how to take action. Chapter 4 defines the security assessment process, describes how it should be approached, and details who should be involved. Chapter 5 probes the components of the assessment process by presenting questions and issues that must be asked when evaluating each component and by explaining how the individual components fit together for effective school security.

Chapter 6 offers an inside view of popular strategies used to improve school security. Although a growing number of schools are implementing these strategies or looking at these issues, many are doing so under false assumptions, based on misinformation and/or without undertaking some key considerations. Likewise, other schools are not implementing these strategies because they are not aware of the benefits to be gained. This chapter looks at some of the pros and cons of various security tactics.

School violence reflects what is occurring in the broader community. As a part of this broader community, schools must work with students, parents, police, businesses, political officials, and other community leaders to develop effective intervention and prevention strategies for maintaining safe schools and safe communities. Chapter 7 identifies issues to consider in this process.

One institution that has significant influence on the progress or lack of progress in improving school security is the media. The media are a major source of fear for many educators. For this reason, Chapter 7 also provides tools for school officials to use in working effectively with the media while still dealing effectively and proactively with school security issues.

Practical School Security is not theory-based or reference-driven. It is not a detailed manual on how to establish school security departments and it does not offer "quick fix" solutions (that generally do not work). It is also not intended to serve as legal advice. Readers should always consult their attorneys prior to implementing security policies, procedures, and programs.

It is, however, intended to meet the demand for an easy-to-read introduction for the many educators and members of the broader school community who have never been exposed to dealing specifically with security in elementary and secondary schools. It offers this exposure from the perspective of a veteran frontline school security professional, not an educator who also deals with school security or a law enforcement officer who works with schools in addition to his other primary duties. This fresh perspective provides inside information that many school administrators may not be aware of and will, I believe, have a positive impact both on the security of schools and the profession of school security.

No endeavor such as this occurs in isolation. I proudly acknowledge my parents, Robert and Frances, for setting the tone for my personal development and professional achievements leading to this book. Likewise, I acknowledge my love and respect for my wife, Candy Rodriguez-Trump, for being my best supporter and my biggest critic.

Thanks to my mentors, peers, and colleagues who have guided me, directed me, and most important, tolerated me in very difficult times: John Fechko, Ron Huff, Mary Lentz, Linda Schmidt, Mike Walker, Jim Zielinski and others too many to name, but all knowing that they hold a special place in my thoughts. Likewise, thanks to those who have intentionally made some times difficult for me. You have solidified my integrity, strength, and determination to forge ahead—qualities anyone committed to the safety of children must possess and treasure.

Finally, my appreciation to Ann McMartin of Corwin Press for her patience and understanding during some very turbulent times that coincided with the development of this book. Her persistence and commitment to her profession contributed greatly to the completion of this work.

About the Author

Kenneth S. Trump is President and Chief Executive Officer of National School Safety and Security Services, a school security and public safety consulting firm in Cleveland, Ohio. He served 3 years as assistant director of a federally funded antigang task force for three Cleveland suburbs, where he was also director of security for the ninth largest Ohio school system. In addition to being an adjunct assistant professor of criminal justice at Ashland University, he served 7 years with the Cleveland Public Schools' Division of Safety and Security, where he designed and supervised its nationally recognized Youth Gang Unit.

Trump received a master's degree in public administration and a bachelor of arts degree in social service (criminal justice) from Cleveland State University. He has extensive training in gangs, violence, and school security topics, including from the National School Safety Center, Federal Law Enforcement Training Center, California Gang Investigators Association, Midwest Gang Investigators Association, and National Association of School Safety and Law Enforcement Officers.

Trump has consulted in 30 states and in Canada on youth violence, gangs, and school security. He has served as an instructor at the FBI National Academy and for the U.S. Department of Justice, National School Boards Association, National School Safety Center, and hundreds of schools, criminal justice agencies, and professional associations nationally.

In addition to being cofounder and vice president of the Midwest Gang Investigators Association (Ohio Chapter), Trump served for six years as a member of the Board of Directors of the National Association of School Safety and Law Enforcement Officers. He authors frequent publications and appears often in the media. Trump has received numerous awards for his contributions to the school security profession and to public service.

PART

I

Myths and Realities
of School Violence

Effective school security does not rank next to rocket science in complexity. Nonetheless, it should in importance. No one can dispute the need for secure schools nor the negative effect of security threats on the educational process.

Unfortunately, efforts and rhetoric associated with enhancing school security are much more complicated than necessary. Whereas the issues need to be examined beyond their surface level, typically good school security is often pushed aside owing to lack of awareness, denial, overreaction or "paralysis by analysis." Far too often, politics, images, and misconceptions of the problems and strategies take a front seat to actual school security.

School officials must take several critical steps before considering specific programs or security techniques to employ in educational settings.

1. Comprehend the real school security threats that challenge educators and safety officials.

2. Establish an environment where political concerns will take a backseat to school security.

3. Establish a common agreement on how to reduce security risks in a rational, effective, and timely manner.

Then, and only then, can our claimed commitment to "zero tolerance" become reality.

There has to be an understanding of the myths and realities of school violence to reach a common agreement on how to reduce security risks. Chapters 1 through 3 identify the major myths that often block effective school security. These myths are frequently perpetuated by the media, expressed by attendees at school security workshops, and communicated by parents who are concerned about the safety of their children in school.

Compare the myths to reality. Then do a reality check on how these issues are viewed and handled in your school or district.

1

Threats to Safe and Secure Schools

Distinguishing Security From Safety

Myth: An audit by insurance carriers or other staff unfamiliar with security adequately identifies school safety problem areas.

Reality: Insurance or other auditors of schools frequently focus on safety from an accident prevention perspective rather than safety from a security perspective.

Although *safety* and *security* are often used interchangeably, it is important to conceptualize them as two different areas. Safety should be viewed as including such traditional concerns as accident prevention, playground and physical education equipment safety, shop class injury prevention, and related matters. Security focuses more on criminal and severe misbehavior responses and prevention, crisis preparedness, physical security, personnel and internal security, and related issues.

Reality check: Does your school conduct traditional safety inspections and nontraditional security assessments to provide a comprehensive picture of overall school safety in the broader meaning?

Traditional Security Problems

Myth: Security problems have always existed in schools, and administrators are experienced in properly handling these problems.

Reality: Whereas certain types of security problems have become a part of "normal" operations in some schools, they are not always thoroughly handled.

Educators are accustomed to such traditional security problems as vandalism, fighting, trash can fires, and one-on-one assaults. Whereas the number of these types of incidents is growing in some schools, most experienced administrators and staff feel relatively comfortable in responding to these security problems. In some schools, these types of issues are viewed simply as a part of the "daily routine."

Although these incidents are considered "routine," there are still some fundamental problems with how they have been handled in many schools. Most administrators adequately dish out such appropriate disciplinary action as suspension, expulsion, and related action for "traditional" offenses. Inadequacies arise, however, when criminal offenses are handled administratively with discipline but not processed as a crime with the involvement of law enforcement.

For example, the high school "bully" decides to shake down a fellow student in shop class for a dollar. After being threatened with bodily harm if he or she does not give the bully a dollar, the student gives in and turns over the money. This happens several times a week for 3 months until the victim's father finds out that his child has not had lunch because the lunch money was being given to the bully.

The father reports the incident to the assistant principal, who investigates and finds that the incidents indeed occurred. The "bully" is suspended and referred for expulsion. Was the problem handled? Yes and no.

The problem was handled administratively with disciplinary action. Nevertheless, such an offense could also be classified as "extortion," a felony in many states. So although the administrator took disciplinary action, he or she failed to address the criminal aspect by notifying the appropriate law enforcement authorities. In short, the administrator failed to report a felony.

Although this issue is addressed in greater detail in Chapter 2, it serves to illustrate here that schools have not always handled traditionally "simple" security problems in the appropriate manner. To adopt a blanket assumption that, "We have always had security problems, so there is no need to be more concerned about it now," is to base an important position on a false assumption in many schools.

To leap to the conclusion that, "We have always handled security problems, so we can handle anything else that comes along," is an equally false assumption.

Reality check: Examine your school operations. Are administrators and staff trained to recognize criminal offenses? Do administrators distinguish crimes from noncriminal, disruptive youth behavior? Do administrators process crimes administratively with disciplinary action *and* criminally by reporting such offenses to the police?

The "Top 5" Issues

Traditional security problems such as those described earlier are not rattling the cages of most educators or parents. What aspect of school violence is capturing attention in the United States? The "Top 5" include the following:

1. Aggressive and violent behavior
2. Drugs
3. Weapons
4. Gangs
5. "Stranger danger"

These issues receive significantly more attention and concern than vandalism or one-on-one fights and assaults.

Aggressive and Violent Behavior

Myth: Incidents of school violence almost always involve drugs, gangs, or related underlying issues.

Reality: Whereas drugs and gangs account for far too many incidents of school violence, the average educator is equally, if not more, concerned about increases in general aggressive and violent behavior that may not be drug or gang related.

Contrary to public perception, gangs and drugs are not the only motivators behind aggressive and violent student behavior. Three factors that incite many students to violence are the following:

1. "He said, she said" rumors
2. Boyfriend or girlfriend changes, disputes, or rumors
3. "Dissin'" (disrespecting), real and perceived

Educators cannot ignore the potential for any of the three factors to escalate to assaults, large-scale fights, use of weapons, or other violence.

In fact, these three factors themselves often ignite gang-related violence. For example, data from the Youth Gang Unit of the Cleveland Public Schools (Cleveland Board of Education, personal communication, December, 1993) revealed that approximately 75% of the school gang-related incidents involved assaults, threats, fighting, menacing, trespassing on school property, and disruptive behavior. Often, the assaults, gang fights, and related disturbances originated from rumors or "dissin'" rather than drugs or other causes often attributed to gang violence.

Gang-related or not, these incidents suggest that school staff need to follow up on resolving "small problems" while they are relatively small. Still, these conflicts are often dismissed by school personnel as "trivial" matters until a situation explodes. It is easier to mediate a two-person dispute at 7:30 A.M., school opening, than to break up a 100-student riot at 2:30 P.M., dismissal time.

Myth: Bullying is not a significant issue in the "big picture" of school security concerns. As the saying goes, boys will be boys (and equally appropriate today, girls will be girls).

Reality: Bullying warrants attention from educators, beginning at the elementary level. The fear, intimidation, and victimization associated with bullying do influence school security.

Education and law enforcement "war stories" are growing with examples of how bullying victims are taking matters into their own hands after a period of victimization. For example, an elementary student is harassed, slapped around, and punched almost daily on the bus ride home from school. After 2 years of abuse, the student brings a knife to school and pulls it out to stab the "bully" when he or she harasses the student on the bus. The potential outcome: a stabbing or a murder stemming from bullying.

School crime problems associated with bullying may include assault, extortion, menacing, sexual offenses, and many other potential actions the bully may choose to take while he or she has control over the victim through psychological or physical intimidation. These behaviors—assault, extortion, menacing, and sexual offenses—are crimes, not "boys will be boys" disciplinary matters. Those who believe otherwise need only ask, "Would I tolerate such victimization as an adult staff member?" Of course not. Then why should students be subjected to the same victimization?

Again, the importance of dealing with "small problems" while they are "small" cannot be overstated. Today's bully is easily tomorrow's gang member. The only difference is that tomorrow the individual bully will be with a gang of other bullies. And they will be "bullying" with weapons and gang violence.

Myth: Violent student behavior cannot be prevented.

Reality: In some cases, violent student behavior can be prevented. Not all incidents can be prevented or predicted, but some can, and the risk of others can be reduced.

What has really focused attention in the United States on increased student violence and aggression? In addition to the younger ages of victims and perpetrators, and their more frequent use of weapons, a progression in the type of violence and aggression has generated increasing alarm. This includes a change from student crimes against (a) property (vandalism, arson, etc.) to (b) students (fights, assaults, stabbings, and shootings) to (c) adults (students assaulting, stabbing, and shooting school employees, parents, police, and other adults).

Destruction of property by students is a problem. Attacks on students by other students is unacceptable. But when student violence is directed at adults, we have a *serious crisis.*

The reality is that problems reach the priority list when they hit home. Violence may be a general concern for everyone, but it is the number one concern when *I* am the victim or potential victim. The United States is a society of, "What's in it for me?" When *it* is one's own safety, the priority level for addressing the issues rises significantly.

Reality check: Does your school staff address all forms of aggressive or violent student behavior in a firm, fair, consistent, and timely manner? Do staff responses to "small problems" communicate to students a level of importance that can serve as a deterrent to their committing more serious offenses? Does your district address the issue of bullying, beginning at the elementary school level? Does your school promote a culture of constructive conflict resolution to avoid student aggression and violence? Does your staff solve problems (staff to student and staff to staff) modeling the same conflict resolution behavior they expect from students?

Drugs

Myth: Kids sell drugs only for the money.

Reality: Money plays a big role in motivating kids to sell drugs. But it is not the only factor.

Youths sell drugs for a variety of reasons and money is, indeed, one of them. U.S. culture defines success by the dollar. Should it be any surprise that U.S. youths have adapted this definition to mean, "Money by any means, including illegal"?

Besides the money, another consideration is the image of the drug dealer. Students hold today's "dope boy" or "dope girl" image—that is, saggin' pants, excessive jewelry, expensive athletic wear, pagers, cellular phones, and money, in much higher esteem than the straight-A student who is dubbed a "nerd" or a "geek." A quick look at the image of drug dealers in the media provides insight into why students, including those who are not drug involved, are adopting this image. Educators, police, and other adults particularly fall prey to this false stereotype when using student appearance (dress, jewelry) as a sole indicator of a drug dealer or gang member.

Myth: School officials are adequately trained on drug issues.

Reality: Overall, schools have done an above-average job in training their staff on recognizing indicators of drug use and abuse. Nevertheless, they take few steps, if any, to train staff to recognize indicators of drug sales or possession. School officials also are poorly informed on the changing nature of drug trends in the communities they serve, even though their lack of information has a direct detrimental effect on their students and, potentially, their school security.

Most educators think of drugs in terms of what they see on television or in other media. It might be the six o'clock news story about crack in a neighboring community. It might be a documentary on marijuana on a prime-time news show. Does this mean that crack and marijuana are necessarily the current drugs of choice in the world of their students? Absolutely not.

Drug trends change from community to community and over a time within the same community. Crack may be the drug of choice today in one community, whereas LSD tops the list in an adjacent town. Educators should be briefed, by law enforcement officials or school security professionals at least twice each school year, on current drug use and trafficking trends in the broader community, particularly as it relates to juvenile drug crime.

Educators also should avoid getting locked into perceiving one such type of drug as crack, as the only drug on the market. Although crack may be a big problem at a given time, it is important to remember that there are many other illegally sold drugs available to students. These may include marijuana, LSD, heroin, methamphetamine, inhalants, Ritalin, prescription and over-the-counter medicine, the now-popular "date rape" drugs, and alcohol. A tunnel vision approach when considering drug trends only decreases one's effectiveness in early recognition, intervention, and prevention of problems.

For example, one principal was amazed when several female students were found in possession of cigars. "I can't believe girls are smoking cigars," he declared. The principal was more amazed when a security official informed him of current drug trends with "blunts": cigars stuffed with marijuana and potentially laced with cocaine, PCP, or even embalming fluid!

Likewise, tunnel vision on drug possession, concealment, and trafficking can be equally paralyzing. Many school officials, for instance, believe that drug dealers are always drug users. This is not necessarily the case. Far too many examples exist of athletes, students on the honor roll, or low-profile students selling drugs. Who better to hold or sell drugs in school than the student least likely to be suspected?

School officials need to be aware of modern tactics in drug concealment and trafficking. The days of "Johnny, empty your pockets," to find suspected drugs, weapons, or other paraphernalia, are long gone. Today drugs are concealed in shoes, socks, jackets, underwear and other clothing, and in bookbags, fanny packs, concealed areas in and around school buildings, and in just about any other potential location within the realm of imagination. Although this issue will be discussed further in Chapter 6, school officials should remember that the absence of drugs in a suspected student's pockets does not guarantee that there are no drugs somewhere on or near the student.

Reality check: Do your school officials tend to focus only on certain students or groups of students as possibly being drug involved based on their appearance and history of being in trouble, or do they consciously monitor for such activity by any student? Has your school staff received training by law enforcement officers or school security professionals on recognizing drug trafficking techniques and trends at least twice a year?

Weapons

Myth: All schools are filled with gun-toting students.

Reality: A small percentage of all students carry weapons. Of those weapons found in schools, fewer guns are usually reported than other types of weapons.

No school news captures public and media attention more than an incident involving a student with a gun. Although one gun in a school is one too many, equally urgent attention needs to be given to other types of weapons. Consider knives, razors, box cutters, metal knuckles, chemical irritants (mace, pepper spray), and the many other items that can be used as weapons.

Educators need training by law enforcement or school security specialists on the different types of concealed weapons. This will broaden their concept of *weapons* beyond guns and knives.

Myth: The majority of incidents that involve weapons used in schools are premeditated over an extended period of time before the actual incident.

Reality: Although it is not uncommon for students to plan to use weapons in schools, a significant number of violent school incidents that involve weapons occur without weeks, days, or sometimes even minutes of advanced planning.

Students carry weapons to school for a variety of reasons. Some students have them for protection while walking to and from school in dangerous neighborhoods. Others bring them for security, in response to such real or perceived threats as intimidation and bullying. Yet others carry them for power, status, or as a tool of their trade (gang or drug business).

Whereas the reasons for carrying them may vary, the use of weapons tends to stem largely from an aggressive response to shame or embarrassment. It is a situation of "You dis' me, I'll dis' you back by shooting you" ("dis'" means disrespect). This disrespect comes in the form of threats, intimidation, humiliation in front of others, or physical assault, especially to get even after being "jumped" by several offenders.

Reality check: When your school officials talk about dealing with weapons in school, do they focus only on guns, knives, or one specific type of weapon? Has your staff been trained by law enforcement, school security, or both specialists on the different types of concealed and visible weapons used by youth? Does your school deal with minor conflicts in a timely and effective manner to prevent escalation that may involve the use of weapons? Do staff members think ahead to prevent retaliation for group, gang, or other similar offenses? Do educators promote a culture of respect by students and staff to reduce the potential for violence stemming from real or perceived disrespect?

Gangs

Myth: There have always been gangs, including gangs in schools. It is no different now than in the past. The problems should be viewed in terms of each individual incident, not in terms of a "gang" problem. If gangs are not officially recognized, they will eventually go away.

Reality: Gangs today are different from gangs of the past, especially those of several decades ago. Although discipline and criminal action should be determined on a case-by-case basis, the overall gang issue should not be dismissed. Denial of a gang presence in schools will exacerbate, not eliminate, the problem or the potential for a problem.

Gangs are a reality today in many urban, suburban, and even rural schools. Gang-related incidents differ from nongang offenses in that they (a) involve a larger number of students, (b) are retaliatory in nature and escalate much more quickly than nongang incidents or a one-on-one conflict, and (c) frequently involve intense violence, the use of weapons, or both.

Although a one-on-one fight or assault may likely end after the first staff intervention, gang-related fights or assaults can escalate from an initial two-person conflict to a large scale riot with weapons within hours (or sometimes minutes). To address gang conflicts as separate, isolated incidents without assessing and addressing the overall gang-related nature of the conflicts increases the risk of continued security problems.

It is wise, however, to give no positive reinforcement to gangs. Gangs, unlike other student groups or organizations, are involved in antisocial, criminal, or both activities. Gangs should not be viewed, classified, or described as clubs, social organizations, or other legitimate student groups. There is no such thing as a "positive" gang.

Although this seems like good common sense, it is not unusual to hear of cases in which school officials give an unbelievable amount of credibility to gangs. For instance, administrators in at least two separate school districts went as far as to hire acknowledged gang members to provide security services in their schools. When these "security" personnel in one school used ganglike violations to "discipline" students, including beatings and up to $100 fines, the programs quickly fell apart.

Not only did this open the school system to an enormous potential for liability, it also gave an incredible amount of status to an undeserving group. Fortunately, both programs came to the attention of the public and raised questions, scrutiny, and serious recognition of not only questionable operational practices but also of the overall issue of giving enhanced credibility to gang members. Considering the trend of gang members toward attempting to portray themselves as legitimate "community-oriented" organizations, school administrators would be wise to closely scrutinize proposals before jumping into programs such as those described earlier.

Myth: Gangs are a community problem, not a school problem.

Reality: Gangs are indeed a community problem. Nevertheless, the schools are a part of the community and, as such, reflect the problems of that community as much as they do the positive aspects. Although schools do not necessarily create gangs, school officials do have a responsibility to do their part in recognizing, addressing, and preventing gang problems.

In years past, Friday was fight day at school. Rumors and conflicts built up all during the school week. After school on Friday, it was on: fight time!

Today, Monday morning is fight time. Conflicts from weekend parties, athletic events, community festivals, unsupervised activities, and other unresolved neighborhood altercations spill over into the schools. After all, if youths cannot get to their rivals to resolve the problem on Friday or Saturday night, they know where everyone will be on Monday morning: in school!

As a school official, can you ignore the 7:30 A.M. fight or riot, even though it did not start in your school? Certainly not. Children and staff concerned about their safety simply will not be able to focus on educational experiences in the classroom.

In some situations, schools also can be selected by gangs as their turf. *Turf* has a completely different meaning today than it did 20 years ago. It is no longer limited to a neighborhood street or community boundary. The mobility of children today results in gang *turfs* being schools, neighborhood recreation centers, malls, and just about anywhere else they choose, if adults allow it.

In some larger school districts, gangs have intentionally abused open enrollment and student transfer procedures to dominate particular schools. Members of a gang scattered throughout the city will intentionally create reasons to request transfers or reenroll in a particular school in which they have a large representation of fellow gang members. After all, gang members want to be "safe" in school!

This type of manipulation can easily go undetected. School administrators need to closely monitor student transfer and enrollment requests, particularly when they suspect student gang involvement. Coordination between building and central office administrators is critical to prevent gang dominance through transfer and enrollment abuse.

Gangs can have a tremendous impact on schools and, therefore, cannot be ignored. In addition to the violence, intimidation, and related disruptions, there is also a dollar cost. Certainly, no administrator prefers to see hundreds or thousands of dollars spent each school year on replacing or repairing school property that has been stolen, vandalized, or damaged by gang graffiti. The time and money spent on dealing with gangs in school can be much better allocated as classroom resources.

Myth: Local students are not really gang members. At best, they are "wannabes" and, therefore, are not a real security threat. If there are no clear signs of gang members, there are no gang problems.

Reality: Students do not have to come from Los Angeles, Chicago, or other large cities to be gang members. The term *wannabe* furthers denial by creating the false perception that students are simply dressing like gang members or calling themselves gang members. Gang identifiers are not always blatant but, instead, they may be low-profile and not easily recognized by the untrained educator, police officer, parent, or other adult.

Academicians, law enforcement officers, educators, and many others continue to struggle with defining the term *gang*. There is no accepted common definition, even after years of debate. Educators need to focus on gangs as groups of adolescents or young adults who are frequently and deliberately involved in illegal activities, whether perpetrated individually or collectively. Gangs share a common identity often expressed by gang names, signs, symbols, and turfs.

Gang members cross all boundaries of age, sex, race, academic achievement, and economic status. There is no "stereotypical" gang member. Gangs are in urban, suburban, and rural communities, and in schools. They are male and female. They are "A" students and students who are failing classes.

There is no one reason why youths join gangs. Gang membership, like drug-related activities and other crimes, is a symptom of broader social and economic societal problems. Motivating factors for children and youths to join may include power, status, security, family substitute, friendship, love, and/or economic gain.

Gangs in school are usually not "transplants" from major cities who are trying to start a "franchise" gang operation. In most cases, they are local kids who are using the signs, symbols, and behavior of gangs that they have learned about in the various media, from relatives in cities with gang problems, or from other sources. School officials often use this argument to classify youths who identify themselves as gang members as really being "wannabes." They must remember, however, to focus more on behavior than on appearance and name. As the saying goes, "If it walks like a duck, talks like a duck and acts like a duck, it's a duck." There is no difference between a gang member in Los Angeles who is dealing drugs, stealing guns, and assaulting students, and a gang member in Ohio who is also dealing drugs, stealing guns, and assaulting students.

School officials also do not go home on Friday and suddenly find an entrenched gang problem when they return to school on Monday morning. Gang development is a process, not an event. Communities and schools may have chronic gang problems or just an emerging gang presence. Clearly, an emerging gang problem that goes unaddressed will soon be an entrenched, chronic gang problem.

As previously stated, a focus on behavior is critical. Nevertheless, recognition of gang identifiers helps educators detect an emerging gang presence in its early stage so they can more effectively prevent the negative behavior associated with gangs. These identifiers may include one or more of the following:

1. Graffiti: unusual signs, symbols, or writing on walls, notebooks, class assignments, or gang "literature" books
2. Colors: obvious or subtle colors of clothing, a particular clothing brand, bandannas, jewelry, or haircuts
3. Tattoos: symbols on arms, chest, or body
4. Initiations: suspicious bruises, wounds or injuries resulting from a "jumping in" (Gang initiations have taken place in school rest rooms, gym, locker rooms, playgrounds, and even hallways!)
5. Hand signs: unusual hand signals or handshakes
6. Language: uncommon terms or phrases
7. Behavior: sudden changes in behavior or secret meetings

Administrators should arrange for staff training on gangs, their identifiers, and strategies for gang management in school. Remember that the identifiers serve to help identify gang members in a school. The reduction of these identifiers and the focus on behavior will help reduce gang conflicts in school.

Reality check: Do your school administrators acknowledge the presence or potential presence of gangs, or are they in denial? Does your staff look at the relationship between a variety of "individual" incidents to see if there is a gang connection and, if so, does the staff take steps to prevent future incidents? Do administrators have relationships with police, parents, and the broader community to identify gang and other neighborhood conflicts that could spill over into the schools, particularly from weekend activities? Is your school viewed as a part of the overall community or an "island" of its own? Do administrators consciously monitor student transfers and open enrollment for requests motivated by gang affiliation or similar reasons? Has your school staff received in-depth training and periodic updates on gang identifiers, behavior, and management strategies? Is an emphasis placed on student behavior or only on appearance and surface-level "identifiers"?

Stranger Danger

Myth: Threats to school security from outside the building usually involve total strangers who have "emotional or psychological problems." Schools cannot prepare for or prevent outside threats.

Reality: A significant number of security threats from outside the building involve individuals who are familiar or potentially familiar to school officials. Staff can take some practical steps to reduce threats from these outside sources.

Administrators, staff, students, and parents have a growing fear of violence perpetrated by individuals from outside the school. This fear is realistic to some extent, considering some high profile incidents in which armed individuals, not associated with schools, have shot staff members or taken hostages in schools or on school buses. It is also realistic to say that officials will have quite a difficult time predicting such offenses.

Nevertheless, a greater threat often exists from so-called outside individuals who could be known to school authorities. Violent incidents and security threats have involved the following:

1. Spouses, former spouses, boyfriends, or girlfriends (current or former) who are involved in ongoing domestic conflict with school staff members
2. Noncustodial parents who attempt to remove their children from school against court orders
3. Former employees seeking revenge for termination or current employees seeking revenge for disciplinary action
4. Trespassing students from other schools seeking to harm students who are attending school, possibly in retaliation for gang incidents, or drug disputes

It is possible for administrators to anticipate violence involving each of these situations if they have adequate information, consciously recognize the potential for a problem, and take general steps to reduce security risks from outside threats. For example, staff members should be informed and reminded during the school year to advise administrators if they fear any potential spillover of domestic situations into the school. Students should be warned, counseled and advised on problems involving individuals from outside their school. Workplace violence training should be provided to enhance staff members' ability to manage and prevent violence stemming from hostile employees. Chapter 5 will also address access control strategies, crisis preparedness, and other issues related to reducing risks from outside of the school.

Reality check: Does your school have adequate access control and visitation procedures? Are staff members and students trained to alert administrators about potential problems by individuals from outside the school? Has your district trained school officials on workplace violence?

New Times, New Crimes

Myth: Experienced educators have seen it all. The problems will always be the same, just with different players.

Reality: Experienced educators have likely seen a great deal in their careers. Many problems do repeat themselves over the years as new kids try old tricks. Nevertheless, educators must be conscious of constant changes outside the school and anticipate how that could influence security in the educational setting.

New times do bring new crimes. It is logical to expect that the "Top 5" security problems previously highlighted will continue to grow in scope and severity. Now, however, additional concerns remain. Crimes and disruptions likely to increasingly threaten school security in coming years include these:

1. *Bomb threats and bombs.* As domestic terrorism threats increase, it is reasonable to expect related issues to influence schools. This includes increased bomb threats and actual bombs placed and even made in schools by students. Again, schools reflect the broader society.

2. *Group conflict involving racial and cultural issues.* Sad to say, racial and cultural problems in the United States are not over. As conflicts arise in the broader community, educators can expect similar problems in schools. It is important to remember that such conflicts are not limited to two particular races or ethnicity. The diversity of the United States presents unlimited possibilities in this area, unfortunately.

3. *Computer-related crimes.* The potential is really significant considering current growth and interest in computers. Computers are already being stolen at alarming rates from schools, largely because of high demand for the product and inadequate security of buildings and equipment. A number of cases involving abuse of school computer services by students (and employees) have also occurred over the past year. Finally, hackers are beginning to realize just how poor system security is for most school computers that, ironically, contain very valuable information, including student records, scheduling plans, personnel data, payroll information, and business and operational data. A person, adult or student, with above-average computer skills and the intention to disrupt, could cause serious damage to school operations.

4. *Sexual harassment and sex crimes.* Sexual harassment has hit many schools and some in a very hard way, including the harassment of gay and lesbian students. Most schools have established policies and procedures to address this issue. Considering the number and younger ages of juvenile sexual offenders, however, it is reasonable to expect incidents of sexual harassment to continue to increase. It is also logical to anticipate the number of such sexual crimes in schools, as rape and sexual imposition, to continue to rise.

Reality check: Does your staff closely monitor local, state, and national news, as well as other resources on security and educational trends, to prepare for future school security threats? Is there a process for staff to share such information and make prevention plans?

It Happened Where?

Myth: Things like "this" can't happen in our schools or communities. It has never happened here before! Those things are for the big city.

Reality: Things like "this"—gangs, drugs, weapons, violence, and other security incidents—can and do happen in urban, suburban, and rural schools and communities. Security concerns no longer should be confined to urban and large suburban districts.

Many people, including school leaders, love to think that, "It can't happen here." When do people want increased airport security? After a bomb or security scare. When do people want increased school security? After a crisis or tragedy occurs somewhere else. Months and sometimes weeks later, everyone forgets and it is back to normal.

School leaders may also allow their personal stereotypes and biases to influence how they view and respond to security. Many falsely believe that issues discussed here do not apply because they live in a predominantly white, suburban community made up of professional-level workers, athletes, and students on the honor roll. But it does happen there, and in all other schools and communities.

The "Politricks"
of School Security

It is important for school administrators to remember that security is different from law enforcement. The American Society for Industrial Security (1996) distinguishes between the two by noting that

> law enforcement focuses on reaction to crime and the enforcement of public laws and ordinances. Security professionals, on the other hand, are more proactive and focus on identifying and preventing a problem before it occurs. In addition, security personnel are more likely to be involved in protecting assets and carrying out an organization's policies and procedures than in enforcing criminal statutes. (p. 3)

Many people conceive of the two as interchangeable when, by definition, they are not exactly the same.

There is also a difference between security and professional security. In relation to schools, the difference is similar to what distinguishes educating from professional education. Parents, siblings, relatives, neighbors, media, and many others educate children in one form or another. Nevertheless, they are usually not certified teachers and such learning is generally not considered as professional education. Just as teachers would take offense at noncertified individuals attempting to teach students in a public school, so too should they take offense at untrained individuals creating and implementing policies and procedures in a school setting under the guise of professional security.

In addition, there is a difference between professional security and professional school security. Although there are many common issues across the professional security field, school security should be viewed as a specialty within the professional security discipline. School districts are unique, and providing professional security services in an educational environment differs from the professional security provided in a hospital, utility plant, corporate office, or other noneducational setting. It is faulty to assume that security is the same in all places. An even more faulty assumption is that a school administrator, law enforcement officer, or hospital security director is a professional school security expert.

"Politricks"—political tricks—is unquestionably the biggest obstacle to having professional school security in many districts. A focus on image, power, control, and money (ironically the same features that motivate many gangs) often takes precedence over reporting crime and implementing professional security measures to truly protect children, staff, and property. This creates varying degrees of denial, rhetoric, underreporting and nonreporting of school-based crime, and a general state of paralysis for those educators, students, parents, and community members who often falsely believe that the people creating this type of environment are actually sincere in their claims of commitment to safe schools.

Denial, Image, and Underreporting

Myth: School security issues are immune from politics and personal agendas. *All* school board members and administrators are *completely* honest in accurately reporting school crime and security concerns to police, employees, parents, and the public.

Reality: Denial, image, and related political motivators play a significant role in how, or even whether, many school officials report school crime and respond to school security needs. Although the phrase "zero tolerance" has gained national use by a substantial number of political and school officials, the action or inaction of many of these individuals fails to place meaning behind the rhetoric.

Every board member, superintendent, and principal is not in denial. Many school leaders are committed and sincere in their concern, talk, and action in enhancing school security. Still, the political problems associated with school security are far too prevalent across the nation.

Denial of security problems by elected and administrative school officials exacerbates security problems and increases the risk of further threats. For example, the scope and effect of denial have been cited as major obstacles to the effective management of gang problems, especially in schools. In his first study of Ohio gangs, Huff (1988) described the effect of denial on schools by noting that

> it is probable that the official denial of gang problems actually facilitates victimization by gangs, especially in public schools. School principals in several Ohio cities are reluctant to acknowledge "gang-related" assaults for fear that such "problems" may be interpreted as negative reflections of their management ability. This "paralysis" may actually encourage gang-related assaults and may send the wrong signals to gang members, implying that they can operate within the vacuum created by this "political paralysis." (p. 9)

Unfortunately, Huff's finding was one of the first of numerous reported concerns about the issues of nonreporting, underreporting, and the lack of data on school-based, gang-related crime across the nation (Kodluboy & Evenrud, 1993; Lal, Lal, & Achilles, 1993; Spergel, 1990; Taylor, 1988).

Similar problems of nonreporting, underreporting, and denial exist with nongang, school-based crimes. Concerns about poor reporting of school crimes and inadequate reporting practices have been cited repeatedly for nearly two decades (Kodluboy & Evenrud, 1993; Quarles, 1993; Rubel & Ames, 1986; U.S. Department of Health, Education, and Welfare, 1978). Yet roughly two decades since the first documentation of the problem, few improvements have been made to establish consistency in reporting across the nation, and the issue of school crime and its associated level of violence has grown to an epidemic-like level of public concern.

A countless number of examples of underreporting and nonreporting of school crimes to law enforcement have been exposed in recent years through news reports, academic studies, law enforcement, reports by school employees and students, after external audits and assessments of school districts, and sometimes, internal audits and subsequent reports. Offenses not reported by school officials range from such property crimes as vandalism, theft, and arson (many involving thousands of taxpayers' dollars), to such crimes against persons and society as assault, drug possession and trafficking, extortion, rape and other sex crimes, weapons possession and use, and much more. About the only offense missing from the examples (so far) is murder!

The exact extent of nonreporting and underreporting is difficult to specify in numbers because there is no central tracking authority for such problems. Nevertheless, increasing indicators of school-crime reporting problems strongly suggest that they are more prevalent than many people would like to believe or admit. It is becoming increasingly difficult for persons to deny this problem, as a national concern, by labeling documented cases of nonreporting as "isolated incidents," "atypical," or "only characteristic of large, urban districts."

For example, a written survey of law enforcement officials who attended a statewide conference in one northeast state found that 61% of the respondents stated that public school officials in the jurisdiction where they work do *not* consistently report crimes that occur in their school(s) and on school property to law enforcement officials. Another 9% stated that they did not know whether crimes were consistently reported by school officials, leaving only 30% who indicated that school officials do indeed consistently report school-based crimes (Trump, 1997a). Whereas this survey represents preliminary findings from a broader study of the issue, it does, particularly for those jurisdictions represented in that survey, raise serious questions about whether school crimes are being consistently reported and, in turn, investigated by law enforcement professionals.

Why do officials fail to report school-based crimes? According to the American Association of School Administrators (1981), the reasons educational administrators refrain from notifying law enforcement officials of school-based crimes include the following:

1. They want to avoid bad publicity, litigation, or both.
2. They fear being blamed for the problem or considered as ineffective in their jobs.

3. They consider some offenses "too minor" to report.

4. They prefer to handle the problems using disciplinary procedures.

5. They believe the police and courts will not cooperate.

Many years after the American Association of School Administrator's report, the reasons for nonreporting remain largely the same.

Far too many cases of nonreporting are intentional and sanctioned by some principals, central office administrators, superintendents, and/or board members. Other instances of nonreporting are less intentional and more a by-product of bad past practices and distortions of outside influences. The reasons for intentional nonreporting include

1. There is fear that if crimes are reported to police, school officials will be perceived by the public as poor managers. Some principals and central office administrators, including superintendents, fear that they will be removed from their positions if it appears that there is "too much crime" in their schools. In some districts, the number of incidents reported has a direct negative effect on administrator performance evaluations and, in turn, on salary increases or continued employment in these positions.

Politricks exist not only between the school system and the community but also within the school system. Even when the data exist, there have been countless examples of manipulation, largely owing to internal competition and the fear of negative consequences to careers (Hill & Hill, 1994). Such behavior exacerbates denial, nonreporting, and an organizational culture focused more on its image than on school security.

For example, some principals submit only selected statistics and information to the central office. Some central office administrators submit only selected statistics and information to the upper administration. And some superintendents "spoon-feed" only selected statistics and information to the board. So even when board members are sincere in dealing with security issues, the information they receive from the administration may be grossly distorted.

2. There is fear by school board members that negative publicity of reported crimes will contribute to their not being reelected to their

positions. Political images and egos are easily bruised. Few bruises are worse than those stemming from the perception by the community that the individuals they elected to the school board have no control over the district.

3. There is fear by school "leaders" that if crimes are reported, parents will perceive the schools as unsafe and remove their children from the school system. A related fear is that if crimes are reported, parents and other voters will not pass school tax proposals for those communities that require funding increases through elections.

4. There is a belief that no data means no problems. If incidents are not reported and data are not collected, then there will be no concrete evidence of a problem. Should the media, parents, or others ask for data or documentation related to school security, administrators can "honestly" say that there are no reports of, or statistics on, such occurrences.

5. There is the issue of control, related to image. Educators are indoctrinated in an environmental culture based on control. Teachers must control their classrooms. Those who are successful in classroom control may be promoted to assistant principals when they are given responsibility for control of discipline in the school. These assistants may be promoted to principals and now would be responsible for controlling the entire school operation. Principals may be promoted to central office positions and would be responsible for controlling an entire school service department. And some will be promoted to superintendent, when they must fully control the entire school district.

The real and perceived need to control, although certainly not the only evaluation factor in determining the promotion of school personnel, can have a detrimental effect on school security. Those who falsely interpret security-related incidents to be a personal loss of control inevitably will make decisions contrary to professional security practices. Nevertheless, those who interpret security-related incidents to be a problem requiring a proactive and preventative response will accurately perceive any inaction as a personal loss of control and, in doing so, will likely pursue proper practices.

In fairness to school administrators, the failure to report crimes can truly be unintentional. Reasons why administrators unintentionally fail to report crimes may include the following:

1. There is a history of school administrators handling all student behavior "administratively" as disciplinary issues. Administrators traditionally have full authority to discipline students for violations of school rules with such consequences as detention, suspension, or expulsion. This is indeed within their realm of authority.

The problem arises, however, when the student "misbehavior" is also a crime. Principals still have the authority to administer disciplinary action within the realm of established policies and procedures. Nevertheless, they also have a responsibility to process the case criminally by reporting the offense to police.

Some administrators falsely believe that by handling the criminal incident administratively, they have fulfilled their obligation. Others inaccurately view handling an incident administratively and criminally as "double jeopardy." Nevertheless, there is no double jeopardy.

Students are not punished twice for the same offense when they are disciplined within the school and reported to law enforcement officials for a violation of the law. Administrators are fully justified—and should be mandated—in reporting crimes to police besides administering disciplinary action. Failure to do so sends a strong message to students that their criminal behaviors are immune from consequences so long as they are committed under the supervision of school officials. This, in turn, increases the likelihood of further criminal behavior.

2. A large number of educators, including administrators, have received little or no training in distinguishing crimes from disciplinary offenses. For example, there is a difference between fighting and assaults. Fighting implies that there are two willing, intentional participants who choose to engage in combat. Assault, however, suggests an intentional act by one individual against a victim who is not inclined to fight. The example in Chapter 1 of the difference between bullying and extortion also provides a perfect illustration.

Although law enforcement, prosecutors, and school security specialists are readily available to provide such training, it appears as though few school personnel see its need or importance until an unreported incident becomes high profile. School administrators should seek this training for themselves and their staff with updates at least once a year. They also should incorporate legal definitions of offenses into their school policies and student handbooks to ensure that school definitions of crimes are consistent with legal codes.

3. Some educators believe that certain crimes are too insignificant for law enforcement to be notified or that they can be better handled "internally" without law enforcement involvement. One of the best examples of this is the occurrence of thefts. School officials have been known to choose to not report thefts of school property, even in cases involving thousands of dollars, because, in their minds, it serves no purpose as their districts are "self-insured." What they seem to forget is that, not only has a felony crime occurred but also that they are self-insured with public taxpayer dollars! Replacement or repair costs for thefts, vandalism, and similar offenses contribute to a significant loss of public dollars that, if prevented, would be better used toward classroom education.

Other administrators are hesitant to involve law enforcement because they fear parental complaints, lawsuits, or both, for their actions. It is not uncommon for central office administrators or board members to provide "less than anticipated" support for principals who take a strong stand when parents complain about discipline or related issues. A lack of central office support discourages principals from firm, fair, and consistent discipline, crime reporting, and security practices when principals know, or perceive, that the district's leaders will reverse their positions when the "squeaky wheel" calls central office to complain.

Law enforcement and criminal justice systems can, at times, contribute to the problem of nonreporting of school crime by school officials. Especially in larger, urban areas where law enforcement and court resources are stretched to maximum capacity, school officials may be unofficially "encouraged" to not report certain such "minor" offenses as possession of small amounts of marijuana or other misdemeanors. By doing so, the police and courts imply that school officials are creating an unnecessary burden by calling the police, leading school administrators to avoid reporting other offenses that they may interpret as "minor." Problems then arise, because school administrators generally do not have the training, experience, or legal right to judge which crimes should and should not be reported.

Reality check: Do your school officials deny the existence of security problems or downplay the potential for problems? Have examples come to light of nonreporting of crimes by school administrators? Do parents and other community members send a consistent message to school leaders that they hold them accountable for open, honest, and accurate handling of school crimes? Do parents and community members take action against school officials for nonreporting, rather than punish them for reporting crimes? Are reporting and data collection within the school system mandated by policies with clear procedures for doing so? Do board members require a regular, standard report on school security from their superintendent, and does the superintendent require such reporting from school administrators? Are there consequences for nonreporting? Have school officials been trained to distinguish crimes from disruptive behavior? Are crimes processed administratively and by law enforcement?

Reality, Not Rhetoric

Myth: Politricks is a part of doing business, in education as well. The effect of school politics on safety and security is minimal.

Reality: Administrators must establish a strong foundation that includes the consistent reporting of school crimes to law enforcement before new policies, procedures, and programs can be developed to enhance school security. Without this foundation, the school house will suffer major structural damage and eventually may even fall. The millions of dollars currently pumped into school violence prevention and intervention programs are largely wasted when these programs are conducted in disruptive and threatening environments where students and staff are focused on their safety, not academic performance and the support programs.

Most people on the front lines do know what is going on in the schools, even in the absence of formal reporting mechanisms and data. It is false to think that members of the school community live in isolation and do not know that crimes occur in school. Similarly false is the perception that the community will perceive school leaders as poor managers if they report crimes.

The reality is that they will be perceived as poor managers for not reporting crimes and for not handling problems head-on. It is then that parents might not pass tax proposals or might move out of the system. Administrative inaction, not action, will eventually lead to their downfall on security issues.

The failure to report school-based crimes and to deal with security matters proactively has negative consequences on several levels. Most important: It is not good for kids. It is wrong! Regardless of the perceived benefits of nonreporting, the reality is this:

1. It teaches children that there are no repercussions for committing criminal acts.
2. It sends a message to students that schools are islands of lawlessness where the criminal laws of the broader community do not apply, thereby subjecting the school to even more potential offenses.
3. It states to the parents and community members that there is a lack of concern about the safety of their children.
4. It states to school employees that there is a lack of concern about the safety of their workplace.
5. It contributes to an atmosphere in which teachers cannot teach and children cannot learn at their maximum capabilities.
6. It creates an inadequate knowledge base regarding the true extent and nature of crimes committed in school and on school grounds across the United States, thereby reducing our ability to develop effective intervention and prevention strategies.

Veteran school security specialists and law enforcement officers are not the only professionals finally talking publicly about the seriousness of this basic tenet of professional security. In its report titled *Risks to Students in School*, the Office of Technology Assessment (OTA) for the U.S. Congress (1995) cited the lack of data on school-related injuries, noting that information had not improved much since 1985. The report concluded:

Definition inconsistencies, the lack of accurate baselines, underreporting, and the absence of a national—and, in most cases, state-level—surveillance system complicate the characterization of trends in injuries at school and undermine public health intervention efforts to stem the impact and severity of risk factors related to school injuries. (p. 108)

The OTA's finding reinforces the position that many U.S. schools have bypassed the first step of acknowledging, reporting, and identifying security problems. One can only ask how these officials attempt to create policies, procedures, and programs to address a problem that they allege does not exist!

Sad to say, the phrase "zero tolerance" has become a political buzzword in many communities. Given the politics of school security, the repeated abuse of such sayings as "new zero tolerance programs for drugs, weapons, and gangs" should be followed with a simple question from students, staff, parents, and the community: What percentage of tolerance did the school system previously have for drugs, weapons, and gangs? 70% tolerance? 50% tolerance? 25%? In short, zero tolerance should be a basic philosophy reflected in school discipline and crime reporting at all times, not a "new" program or political rhetoric.

Reality check: When someone uses the phrase "zero tolerance" at your schools, is there action behind the words? What concrete steps are being taken to demonstrate zero tolerance? What are your crime-reporting procedures? Is this information readily available to members of the school community?

Tactics by Political Victims

By consistently and accurately reporting school-based crimes, educators and school security and police officials can reverse the tragic trend of political priorities taking precedence over school security. This step, taken via a national legislative mandate, would send a stronger message to the students, staff, and community that they can expect schools to be the safe and secure havens that they were in the past. Done properly, it can also be a positive public relations tool for the school district.

Unfortunately, political leaders have not been able to see the need, or in some cases, have bowed to the lobbying efforts of those individuals and organizations whose self-interests would be harmed by mandatory school-crime reporting laws. Experience suggests that such legislation is far from being a reality, and even if passed, some school officials will seek a loophole to continue nonreporting. Many well-intentioned students, teachers, support staff, law enforcement, parents, community members, and even media have approached their school officials with this issue with enthusiasm, only to be more beaten down politically than some of the victims of actual school crime are beaten down physically. Every day, parents are charged with child abuse. Yet in many ways, the criminal justice, social service, and education systems are allowed to subject children, teachers, and school staff to the daily abuse of threats of violence without consequences!

Where do the victims of the politricks of school security turn for assistance? Although controversy is not the most efficient method for dealing with an issue, administrators need to realize that students, staff, parents, law enforcement, and other stakeholders who have exhausted legitimate means for addressing school security will turn to other sources for assistance. Having been stonewalled, lied to, and in some cases, politically harassed, some of these individuals have found the following sources supportive:

1. *School employee unions and professional organizations.* These groups have varying levels of influence but can, in many cases, force the hand of school administrators who are unwilling to deal with school security issues. Many unions are including security measures as a part of their bargaining talks and contracts as a workplace safety issue. Others are using aggressive public awareness campaigns, including media statements, that cannot be as easily quashed or politically punished as is done to individuals.

2. *The media.* School violence, unfortunately, gets attractive headlines in newspapers, radio, and television. Alarmist coverage and inaccurate stories harm effective security efforts. Nevertheless, media attention is one of the few things that gets quick action from top administrators and elected officials who are not addressing the problems. When all legitimate efforts have failed, some politically-abused victims, including staff and parents of students, have turned to the media to expose their abuse.

3. *Legal action.* Lawsuits also get the attention of school officials. A growing number of these are focusing on safe and secure schools. Although a substantial number of legal claims against school systems are frivolous, a good number of the security claims are legitimate. If school officials show a deliberate indifference to evidence and concerns clearly placed before them, it is highly likely that a more independent forum, such as a courtroom, may be a last resort to get action.

Lawsuits, media attention, unions, and other political pressures are usually last resort efforts that are used when school officials are not responsive to other reasonable requests to address security concerns. Administrators can avoid these tactics by being progressive and proactive in addressing school security. Logic should prevail, even in highly politicized environments, when dealing with safety and security concerns. All efforts should be made to focus on clear facts, concrete evidence, and balanced, sound recommendations that can be implemented as a school-community team.

3

Safely Managing the Problem

Myth: The political and personal agendas are too overwhelming. These obstacles to improving school security simply cannot be overcome.

Reality: Overall, educators, law enforcement officers, parents, students, and other community members want to "do the right thing" in providing safe learning environments. The political issues described in Chapter 2 present some major obstacles. There will be no "quick fix" solution and no simple "checklist" for putting and keeping everything in its proper place. Rarely will it be easy. But it can be done. And it can be done in a "win-win" manner for all.

Getting on the Same Page

The first step to safely managing the problem is to get everyone on the same page. This is probably the most difficult step. The following is a 5-point continuum on which individuals, organizations, and communities often fall in addressing school security issues:

1. *Lack of awareness.* This is defined as "simply not recognizing a problem or not knowing how to address a problem that is recognized."

2. *Denial.* This "occurs when officials are aware of a problem, and possibly even know an appropriate response to the problem, but refuse to admit that the problem exists."

3. *Qualified admittance.* This is a position by which "the problem is partially recognized and confronted, but only in a limited manner and not to the actual degree to which it needs to be addressed."

4. *Balanced and rational approach.* This "incorporates all three components of prevention, intervention, and enforcement."

5. *Overreaction.* This is characterized as a "point where many people perceive most schools as being filled with gun-toting, drug-dealing gang members who spend their entire school day committing crimes on campus. . . . The resulting tension and hysteria can lead to increased violence by students and to progressively harsher reactions by adults, who respond more to the perception of fear than to the reality of the threats that may actually exist." (Trump, 1997b, pp. 266-268)

The key to successfully getting on the same page is to assess where each key individual and organization falls along this continuum and then to get everyone to adopt a balanced and rational approach. The process of assessing where individuals, organizations, and communities are on the continuum frequently involves the formation of "task forces" or committees, often with duplicate and nonproductive meetings, descriptive assessments or reports, and many times in the end, few concrete steps or products resulting in true security improvements. School administrators need to be aware that this process can consume a great deal of energy, waste time, and what is most important, have minimal effect.

Progress can be made. Understanding different professional and personal perspectives is critical and should be included in the problem identification and assessment process. But a deadline needs to be placed on doing this and then moving on to action. Everyone cannot agree on everything, but they can agree to disagree and move ahead with concrete steps. "Paralysis by analysis" is one of the leading contributors to poor school security, and talking about a problem for the sake of feeling good about talking about it is, in reality, still doing nothing.

Basic Assumptions

There are five basic assumptions critical for dealing with school security:

1. Law enforcement and schools have similar, not competing, goals.
2. Crimes must be handled administratively and by law enforcement.
3. Crime reporting is a positive safety tool.
4. Security is a public relations tool, not a public relations disaster.
5. School safety requires a multifaceted approach. (Trump, 1997b, pp. 270-272)

School and law enforcement officials do have the same goal: safe and secure schools. Whereas they may differ on objectives for reaching this goal, crimes must be reported, and the importance of reporting crimes must be ingrained within the school's organizational culture as a positive tool for developing prevention and intervention programs. Effective school security is also a public relations tool because most students, staff, and parents want secure schools, provided that school measures are balanced with prevention, intervention, and enforcement. These basic principles must be accepted before anyone can move ahead with new policies, procedures, and programs to improve school security.

Community Ownership

Collective ownership of the problems of school violence and the solutions, including security enhancements, is the only way to effectively manage this issue. Schools alone do not create violent children; nor do police departments, social service agencies, community centers, or political bodies. But all of these entities—and many others—must deal with the final outcome.

Any of these individual agencies or their members will have little success with taking public ownership of the problems or efforts to control the problems by themselves. They will quickly realize minimal success of their policies, procedures, and programs, and increase their political liability as the problems continue to grow and the community looks to those who took sole ownership for answers. In short, it is programmatic and political suicide to try to take them on alone.

The key stakeholders must collectively and publicly acknowledge the problems as a community problem. These stakeholders include representatives from schools, law enforcement and criminal justice, social and other youth service providers, political entities, businesses, churches, neighborhood groups, media, parents and— most important—children and youths. None of these groups alone created the problems, but they all must deal with them.

Community collaborations have been quite popular in the past 5 years. Progressive leaders have realized that shared ownership can lead to shared success. Funding sources for youth and other programs are even mandating collaboration before they will fund many projects.

Collaboration is great when it is sincere and results in action. Problems arise, however, when all stakeholders mentioned earlier get together for a press conference and do damage control after high-profile incidents and create the false perception that they are doing something for the right reasons when, in reality, it is all a smoke screen. If collaboration exists for developing such a final, concrete product as improving school security, then great. If collaboration exists for political reasons or because it is the popular thing to do, and all that results is rhetoric, then administrators should focus their energies elsewhere on more productive tasks!

Tools for Balance

Chapter 7 identifies 10 basic services a good school-community collaboration can provide to reduce juvenile crime and improve school security. These 10 general service areas or roles need to be operationalized by individual communities and schools on the basis of the problems at that point in time and the potential problems anticipated for the future. But how do you get everyone on the same page and how do you stay focused?

Five simple tools, along with strong leadership, can help maintain focus and prevent stakeholders from falling into the counterproductive positions of lack of awareness, denial, qualified admittance or overreaction. These include the use of the following resources.

Concrete Data and Facts

Facts, figures, and case studies must be assembled, and in some cases, be indisputable to reduce the risk of stakeholders resting on preconceived notions or posturing on political platforms. Even with data and facts, it can be difficult to persuade people to move forward with a security program. Without data and facts, it will be even more difficult.

What are the sources of data related to school security? Some include:

1. *Police calls for service to schools.*

2. *Police offense or incident reports for schools.* (Note that this may be different from Number 1 Police may be called to schools, but a report may never be made as a result of the call.)

3. *Security incident reports.* School security personnel, administrators, and staff should complete standard incident reports for security-related incidents and offenses. Incident reports should be categorized and periodic summaries compiled to analyze data trends. Many schools, even those without security departments, have such forms in place. Those that do not should establish one immediately.

4. *Discipline data.* Most schools regularly compile data on student discipline. Larger school districts have "pupil services" offices or similar departments that coordinate discipline-related services throughout the system. Suspensions, expulsions, and other figures should be available with a breakdown by offense categories.

5. *Federal and state data.* Many states require local districts to report discipline and other demographic data on at least an annual basis. Federal data are also required, including those for grant-

funded programs. Projects falling under such programs as "Safe and Drug-Free Schools" funding, as well as other grant programs in the school system, should be reviewed for data collected and reported in grant applications, evaluations, and reports. The absence of such data usually makes obtaining a grant much more difficult.

6. *Surveys.* Many school districts conduct student, staff, or both types of surveys periodically to assess particular issues. Student surveys on drug use have been particularly common over the past decade and a number of them are now being conducted on violence and safety concerns. Employee unions also survey their members from time to time, a potential source of additional information.

7. *Audits, assessments, and consultant reports.* Government or private audits and assessments may be commissioned for a variety of reasons by school systems. Check to see if state agencies (e.g., education or treasurer offices) or other consultants have been hired to assess issues that might involve data collection or analysis of problems related to school security.

8. *Community reports.* A variety of criminal justice, social services, and other youth service agencies, as well as chambers of commerce, private businesses, colleges and universities, philanthropic foundations, and others conduct studies, assessments, or write reports related to juvenile crime and violence. Although the information may not always be school specific, it will provide insight into community youth safety concerns. As school officials know, the schools reflect the community.

9. *Unions and professional organizations.* In addition to conducting member surveys, a growing number of unions and organizations for school employees are establishing data collection mechanisms to gauge measures related to school security. Some teacher unions are actually requiring teachers to fill out special incident reports so the union can check on school administrators to ensure no statistical manipulation or such "accidental misplacement" of reports and data as underreporting and nonreporting.

10. *Physical evidence, videos, photos, and other visuals.* Nothing beats physical evidence to illustrate a point. Whereas one knife or

five guns may not represent the scope of a particular school security problem, they are always great supplements to illustrate a point. Likewise, videos or photos make a great substitute for the real weapons, drugs, or other paraphernalia.

For example, one suburban school district aggressively denied the existence of a drug problem at one of its high schools, despite repeated complaints from neighbors of drug abuse and trafficking outside the school prior to school opening. One "chronic" complainer, a neighbor who lived on the street behind the high school, started video recording the activity from her living room window at 7:00 A.M. each morning. After security and police officers followed up on 25 separate students involved in drug offenses that were captured on video during a 6-month period, the denial slowed down. (Even so, a few administrators still felt the best way to solve the "problem" was to have the neighbor stop taping!)

11. *Student, parent, and community input.* Involving the stakeholders in the school community helps keep a balanced picture of the problems and required strategies. Ownership of safe and secure school plans on the front end reduces the risk of ineffective plans, lack of support, and negative publicity after the fact.

Several problems may be encountered when trying to locate data. First is the absence of data, suggesting that questions then need to be asked about why data are not collected (no data, no problem?). Second, there may be reluctance, particularly on the part of some school officials, to provide the data. Although these data are usually public information and must be provided on reasonable request according to the law, the benefits of having data outweigh the risks of having to release them because of public inquiry. Partial information or "homogenized" versions of the full reports should not be created in response to these requests simply to paint a better picture of the school, district, or both, than the actual data suggest. Trust and honesty are critical elements of effective collaboration, which could be damaged if school officials attempt to distort reality.

College and University Support

Academic studies are not a substitute for internal school data or professional school security assessments. Nevertheless, research and analysis of data and other information related to school security can help focus more on facts and less on perceptions. Many colleges or universities have education, social service, and/or public administration departments that would be thrilled to design surveys, analyze data, or assist in providing technical assistance to school systems on security and violence prevention. Also, many of these departments will provide this support at minimal or no charges as a part of student projects or internships, saving the school system a great deal of money.

Education Programs for School Personnel, Students, Parents, Community Members, and the Media

People often base opinions on false perceptions or their fears of the unknown. Beyond media stories, many individuals have little knowledge about gangs, drugs, weapons, youth violence, or other school security issues. Schools should regularly provide education programs for all stakeholders to present a balanced understanding of the problems, the rationale behind security measures taken in schools and related information. No school official would disagree that "education is the key," so why should this stop with security issues?

Youth Involvement

The importance of student involvement in identifying security concerns and in making recommendations for corrective and preventive action cannot be overstated. Too often we forget to involve those directly affected by the problems, the students. Not only is their input important but their solutions for dealing with problems are often more creative and practical, and less complex and costly, than those proposed by adults. Student involvement adds a touch of reality and balance to the process.

Professional Security Assessments

Officials frequently attempt to "attack" security problems either haphazardly or with extreme measures. Although it is wise to avoid paralysis by analysis, it is equally wise to have a plan for enhancing school security methodically and logically. Professional school security assessments by school security specialists can provide a blueprint for taking short-term and long-term measures in a rational, balanced and prioritized manner.

Reality check: At what point are you, your organization, and your community on the continuum: Lack of awareness? Denial? Qualified admittance? Balanced and rational? Overreaction? In managing the school security issue, is there common agreement on basic assumptions regarding goals, crime reporting, and related issues? Are your schools part of a collaborative approach to school safety? Are all available resource agencies or persons involved in the process? If so, is this collaboration based on political correctness or action? What data and facts are collected and analyzed in assessing your school's security? Are education programs on school security provided for school personnel, students, parents, community members, and media? Are students involved in your security planning process? Has a professional school security assessment been conducted for your school(s)? If so, are the recommendations used as a blueprint for implementing security enhancements, or are they just stored on the shelf with other reports?

PART

II

School Security Basics

" I 'm an educator, not a cop." These words have been heard often in schools, and they are likely to be heard again in the future. Most educators do not want to be law enforcement officers. The majority did not choose a college major in criminal justice, nor do they now want a "minor" in security services. But they do want safe learning environments for their students and for themselves.

What do you do after brushing up on the myths and realities of school security threats, learning the politics, and understanding how to safely manage the problem? How do you know if you have taken appropriate steps to improve school security? What areas should you address? How do you do it? Or should you be doing it at all?

All of these questions are on the minds of a large number of school administrators and a growing number of teachers, support staff, law enforcement and security officials, parents, and community members. "Tell me what to do," is the statement heard repeatedly at most seminars on school safety. "But tell me the basics quickly and precisely because I'm overloaded as it is," they add.

The remainder of this book attempts to meet this request. Chapters 4 through 7 are short, concise, and easy to read. But they are also loaded with key, basic questions that must be asked and critical issues that must be considered when conducting assessments and implementing some of the more popular strategies turned to today for improving school security.

4

The Security Assessment Process

What Is an Assessment?

The purpose of a professional school security assessment is to provide educational leaders with an audit of existing security conditions within their school or school district and to make recommendations for improving these conditions at the building, district, or both levels. An assessment identifies vulnerabilities and risks related to security threats. It also makes specific recommendations, short-term and long-term, for corrective action to reduce these risks or to continue effective practices.

The assessment must be unique to the school, district, or both being assessed, not be a "canned" package of generic recommendations. It must also reflect more than a mere "walk-through" look at doors, locks, and other physical security features. Anyone who claims to provide a thorough security assessment of a school with just a 15-minute walk-through and no other evaluation methods will most likely not give school officials the best possible product.

Individuals who conduct professional security assessments should clearly indicate the assessment scope and limitations. Information contained in the final assessment report should be consistent with the most current recommendations and practices in the school security field at that time. Even then, school officials should consult with their legal counsel when implementing specific policies, procedures, and programs developed as a result of the assessment.

Although there will be some common areas of agreement, every school security assessment likely will be different. Some districts want in-depth assessments at each school or at selected sites. This type of assessment will be highly specific in terms of security threats and physical security concerns.

Other districts require an assessment of the district. This type often looks at such broader issues as policy and procedure consistency across schools, security staffing needs and operations, political and administrative contextual issues, and school-police-community coordination. School leaders may request a district and a building-specific assessment in which the final report would be all-encompassing.

Because no two assessments are usually the same, even when conducted by the same person, it is important to clearly define assessment expectations and responsibilities at the onset of the process. This is particularly true if an outside consultant or resource is used to conduct the assessment. Regardless of who does the assessment, an ongoing dialogue between assessors and school personnel will be critical.

The assessment should be viewed as a process, not a product-driven inspection. Generally, it should not focus on specific brands of equipment or services from a particular company. The final recommendations may include suggestions for types of corrective measures, but the assessment itself should not be a marketing mechanism for selling products.

Evaluation Methods

Professional security assessments should include analyses of the following:

Security-Related Policies and Procedures. Many districts have detailed policies, others have few or none. Some districts have policies but no corresponding procedures. Far too many have policies and procedures, but they are not reflected in practice.

For example, a few of the more "progressive" districts have established policies that mandate the reporting of crimes and serious incidents in their district. Yet the procedures (or administrative regulations in some systems) provide only vague comments on reporting these offenses to central office administrators. Nowhere do such procedures define a crime, provide a list of crimes, distinguish crimes from disruptive behavior, or identify steps for administrators and staff to take in finding out such information. The result: a nice-looking policy with no practice!

Other districts have volumes of policies and regulations. The problem is that the volumes are stored away in administrative offices and nobody knows they exist. Or security-related policies and procedures are scattered throughout these volumes and administrators are not required to know them until a crisis hits.

For example, in a recent case in one school district, a veteran school security official was indicted for more than a dozen criminal offenses committed outside his place of employment. An investigation found that this individual, who was employed with the district for close to 20 years, had several other criminal convictions prior to and during his period of employment with the schools. In a damage control move, district officials scrambled to fire him using a decade-old policy that required employees to inform their employer of any criminal convictions during the individual's term of employment.

This would have been fine except that administrators had never provided their employees with a reasonable notice of pertinent district policies until that time. In fact, some administrators admitted confidentially that they did not know about the policy. Chances are, the employee, although certainly wrong for his criminal behavior, would have a strong technical argument if his case went to court or to union arbitration.

Structured Interviews, Surveys, or Both. These should be of a cross section of representatives of the school community, including policy makers, administrators, teachers, support staff, students, parents, and law enforcement personnel. Perspectives and security concerns vary across these stakeholder groups, all of which play a key role in building safe schools. Their input on identifying problems and potential solutions is critical.

Interviews unquestionably bring to light things that a walk-through alone, and other limited evaluations, can never reveal. In one vocational school, for example, a security consultant interviewed administrators and staff who were confident that they did not have a drug problem in their school. They did express concerns about theft problems with supplies in auto, wood, and other shops.

Meanwhile, students who were interviewed focused less on the theft problem but stated that there was a drug problem in the school—abuse of inhalants. The final finding of the assessment: Students were stealing glue, butane, and other "supplies" from shop classes for purposes of drug abuse. The school officials had a theft problem that they recognized, but they overlooked a more important underlying drug problem.

Analysis of Crime and Discipline Data. This component should include data from within and outside the school as listed in Chapter 3. It is important to look for increases and decreases in different categories, as well as significant percentage changes in categories over several years that may otherwise not be reflected in raw numbers alone. These figures could illustrate a significant shift in such types of security problems as a shift from property crimes to more crimes against persons.

Examination of Facility Physical Design and Structure. This is important for identifying areas of risk reduction created by such issues as poor lighting, inadequate locks and key control, excessive access points, no perimeter definitions, and inadequate inventory control. School facilities, especially older schools, are designed for disaster, not security. Some physical security changes could be quite costly. Other such simple measures as reducing building access points requires minimal effort or dollars.

The assessment process should consist of as many evaluation methods as possible, given the time and financial constraints associated with conducting the assessment. Student and staff written surveys, review of newspaper clippings related to school security, evaluation of progress made by the school in implementing similar prior recommendations, attendance at school-related meetings, and comparable efforts would contribute to the quality, scope, and depth of assessment information. A good evaluator who knows school security will be able to detect common themes and patterns of concern within a reasonable period of time when looking at multiple information sources.

Without doubt, such single-pronged approaches, as only examining physical security or only reviewing data, provide limited information for making an accurate assessment with practical recommendations that will have a positive effect. Likewise, the "checklist approach" also should be used with caution. Many security checklists or guides published today are incomplete, limited, and/or compiled by individuals lacking experience or knowledge in professional school security.

Who Should Assess?

School security assessments ideally should be performed by individuals with experience in professional school security. They might include school security directors, school resource officers, police officers, or similarly experienced consultants or outside resources. It is important that those conducting assessments be trained, knowledgeable, and experienced with professional security standards and in school environment dynamics.

It is equally important to remember that, whereas the security assessment can be attempted by educators and others, using checklists and fragmented pieces of information from various seminars or reference documents, the outcome will be limited. Simply ask yourself, as a principal, if you would like your custodian to write elementary curriculum, even though your curriculum director gave the custodian a checklist of what to do. Or on a personal note, would you want your carpenter to do your root canal work, even if the carpenter were given a checklist of steps to take by your regular dentist?

Likewise, outside consultants and overnight experts should be scrutinized to avoid getting "packaged" assessments that fail to focus on the uniqueness of individual schools and school districts. Ten years ago, it was not "politically correct" to talk about school security. Although this is still the case in some districts today, the number of self-proclaimed school security "experts" continues to grow. Former educators, administrators, police officers, and others with peripheral affiliations with schools are now eager to sell your district their security "expertise," regardless of whether they have professional education, training or experience in this area.

Can administrators, educators, and other school staff conduct a "self-assessment"? The answer, of course, is yes. Some aspects of good security are common sense and with an appropriate understanding of basic security principles, improvements can be made in self-assessments. Nevertheless, it must be recognized from the onset that the outcome will be much more limited than if the assessment were to be conducted by a school security professional.

Common Pitfalls

Some of the more common mistakes in assessing school security include the following:

1. Failing to distinguish safety from security, as described in Chapter 1
2. Focusing on such "one-shot" approaches as only security equipment, without considering the big picture
3. Relying solely on the checklist approach or comparisons with other districts, without considering the quality of the checklist or the uniqueness of individual schools and districts
4. Assuming that anyone can assess security issues, instead of recognizing and respecting security as a profession and school security as a specialty within the security profession

Currently, there is no "only way" to make security assessments for secondary and elementary schools. There are preferences and debates between even the most experienced school security professionals. Nevertheless, educators should avoid the common pitfalls and closely scrutinize outside consultants, overnight experts, and packaged products to ensure that security assessments performed for their schools include the focus and evaluation methods described in this chapter and that the areas assessed include the components described in Chapter 5.

Benefits of Assessing

The benefits of conducting professional security assessments include these:

1. Identification of such practical strategies as procedural changes, which require minimal to no costs for better safeguarding staff, students, and property
2. Creation of a final report that serves not only as a security planning and implementation guide but also as a strong risk management and public relations tool

3. Demonstration of a commitment to the security of students, staff, and facilities through a professional and methodical review without "paralysis by analysis," overreaction, or panic response to a crisis situation or to legal action

In short, the professional security assessment is a proactive tool for meeting the actual security needs of the school and the political concerns facing average school leaders. Assessments provide a fresh perspective for administrators from one generally not available elsewhere on staff: that of a school security professional. The final assessment report provides administrators with a tool for balanced, rational, short-term and long-term school security planning.

5

Security Assessment Components

M any school officials look only at prevention-oriented curricula or only at security personnel and equipment when considering how to make their schools safe. Although such steps are needed in many schools, a proactive approach requires examination of the entire continuum of options that fall under prevention, intervention, and enforcement strategies. Whereas the traditional approaches to school safety often do not include security issues, educators should ensure that the following components are included as a part of their security assessment.

Security Policies and Procedures

The assessment must focus on whether policies exist for specific security problem areas, which will vary with the times. More important, it must consider whether the policies and procedures are legally sound, comprehensive, practical, and updated. Sound policies must lead to specific procedures that are provided in writing and when training the staff. The mere existence of a security-related policy is of minimal value if it is not reflected in practice. A good assessment should evaluate whether policies lead to procedures that lead to practice!

Specific policies will vary, based on local, state, and federal laws as well as unique needs and circumstances of the particular school district. As a basic starting point, all districts should have policies on the following security-related topics:

- Bomb threats and suspicious device management
- Computer-related offenses, including misuse of school equipment and systems, unauthorized use, tampering or hacking, and Internet abuse
- Criminal offenses, including prohibiting misdemeanors and felony crimes by students and staff. Most districts currently have such policies, especially for possession, use or sale of drugs, and weapons possession or use. These policies should include prohibition of counterfeit drugs and look-alike and toy weapons.
- Crime reporting, internally to a central office and externally to law enforcement
- Electronic communication devices, including prohibition of student possession of pagers, cellular phones, and related devices
- Employee background checks and notification requirements to school officials of any arrests, convictions, or both during the individual's period of employment
- Employee relationships with students, including prohibition of dating, fraternization, sexual relationships, inappropriate touching of students, and related activities
- Gang and group disruptions, including prohibition of gang activity on school property or at school-sponsored events. Although these policies tend to address gang identifiers, it is also important to focus policies on behavior.
- Media relations procedures, including guidelines for the media and school employees during normal operations and crisis situations
- Procedures for students, required by medical order, to take prescribed medication
- Security equipment use or such targeted techniques as metal detectors, surveillance cameras in schools or on buses, drug-sniffing dogs, student searches, and interrogations by law enforcement
- Use-of-force guidelines for staff

- Visitation and access procedures for all school and administrative facilities

Policies should be written to apply on school property, including school transportation units and to such school-sponsored events as athletic events, dances, field trips, and other school-sanctioned activities.

The list above is not all-inclusive, nor should it be. Boards and administrators must be flexible with the times in developing new policies and revising or eliminating old policies, as need warrants. School legal counsel always should be involved in policy development before formal passage. Professional associations representing school boards, administrators, teachers, and other school interests usually have specific recommendations, policy samples, and legal concerns available to share with their members, to assist in policy formulation.

Also, school administrators must look beyond traditional policy and procedure manuals when conducting a school security assessment. Are school policies and procedures clearly delineated in student handbooks? Staff handbooks? Are signature forms on file as a matter of record to prove that each student and staff received a handbook? These are all important assessment questions.

Security Staffing and Operations

Various forms of staffing are being used in schools across the United States to address security needs. There is no single staffing method that is the only and absolute form for all schools. The three most popular personnel options are school security departments, school resource officers and school police departments (Trump, 1997b, pp. 274-277).

School security departments generally consist of in-house personnel with varying levels of authority, depending on the school system and/or state and local laws. They also perform a wide range of functions, varying not only from district to district but also within the same district. The size of these departments can range from one person to hundreds, depending on the size and needs of the school systems.

One positive feature associated with school security departments, provided that they are properly supervised and operated, is the element of school district control over personnel selection and assignments. School security personnel in many districts have a lengthy employment history, offering strong backgrounds, knowledge, and skills in handling school disruptions and crimes. It is also helpful that school security personnel are experienced in dealing with school discipline systems, politics, and bureaucracies that can be challenging for those unfamiliar with these operations.

Negative aspects of school security departments include poor pay, lack of training, and frequent requirements to perform non-security-related duties that are more appropriate for administrative aides than for security professionals. School security departments often have low status in the district's organizational structure, placing them in frequent power-control struggles with other school administrators over professional security procedures and issues. Many times, these departments also lack experienced leadership to provide professional school security services.

The use of *school resource officers* (SROs) as an alternative to, or in addition to, school security staff is another personnel form that is growing in popularity. SROs are usually local or county law enforcement officers assigned by their departments to work in schools within their jurisdiction. Whereas their responsibilities vary, these generally include law enforcement, periodic classroom or other education programs, and/or student counseling related to proper school behavior and the law.

Positive features of SRO programs include having a sworn law enforcement officer at the school with full arrest authority. The street experience of most SROs, along with their training, adds unique perspectives and skills to the school team. Having an SRO in a school benefits both the school and the police department because juvenile crime issues in the schools and in the community are often interrelated.

Difficulties with SRO programs may include financial constraints and politics. Some SRO programs are fully funded by the schools, others by the police department, and many by a sharing of the costs by the two entities. So long as everyone agrees, budgets permit the expenses, and the issue is politically neutral, there should be no problem. A change in any of these three situations can quickly change the form, services, and effect of this program.

Other difficulties may include personnel selection, reporting, and supervision issues. Who selects the SROs—the police department, school staff, or a combination of each? To whom does the SRO member report—a police supervisor, the principal, or both? What if there is a conflict between school and police procedures? These issues can be a potential problem if not addressed on the front end and monitored as the program develops.

School police departments are regular law enforcement entities comparable to city or county police agencies. Many colleges and universities already have such departments in place. Officers from these departments usually have full arrest authority but work full-time for the school district.

Positive features of school police departments include full ownership over the department, with personnel selection and supervision. As full-time school employees, the officers' commitment is fully to school policing for that district. If the pay and benefits for school police officers are comparable to those of other police departments, then the school system could reasonably enjoy a full career of service from many such officers.

Probably the biggest obstacle to this option is that many states currently do not have legislation to authorize such departments. This can be overcome with proper leadership by state legislators, in cooperation with law enforcement and education officials. A handful of states have had school police departments in operation for many years and there are many "lessons learned" to be shared by these districts.

Another issue when considering school police departments involves finances. Police departments have significant budgetary expenses, including costs for ongoing training, equipment, vehicles, and other operational expenses. On the flip side of this issue, any professional security personnel option must have similar costs, especially ongoing training and necessary equipment.

Whereas these three personnel options are the most popular, they are not the only options. Some schools still use the traditional "hall monitor" approach as their "security." A smaller number use contract security, although many security professionals have concerns about this option because of their history for high turnover rates, low pay, poor training, and lack of control over personnel assignments. Others may use a combination of approaches, such as

SROs, in-house security, and periodic contract security for special events.

Many issues need to be evaluated when assessing which form best suits a specific school or district. These include local and state legal parameters, budgetary effect and constraints, school and community standards, and—most important—current and future security threats and service needs. When conducting an assessment, it is important to look not only at current needs but also at what will likely be needed in future years so that assessment recommendations reflect steps to prepare for, and it is hoped, to prevent increased security threats.

Equally important is the need to ensure that, despite the staffing method, duties and responsibilities of security personnel must be clearly focused on performing security functions on a regular and professional basis. One of the biggest problems identified in many security assessments is that individuals hired to perform security functions are often assigned duties and tasks not directly related to security. To have security personnel perform administrative support roles or other nonsecurity tasks routinely subjects the school to significant liability, should an incident occur that could have been prevented, or potentially prevented, if the security official had been doing his or her proper job.

Which security staffing form best suits the current and future needs of the school or district? Are security personnel properly trained and deployed? Are security personnel performing official security functions on a regular basis? Does the security department have adequate policies and procedures to guide their personnel? Is there supervision and leadership by a trained, experienced school security profession or by someone with no experience in this area who also supervises other school services? All these—and much more—should be asked when assessing school security staffing and operations.

Crisis Preparedness Guidelines

Every district and individual school should establish crisis preparedness guidelines. A series of "What if?" questions related to security should be answered and documented in a user-friendly format. Complicated, detailed crisis plans may be appropriate for select administrators, but staff need a quick reference to such guidelines as a bullet-type checklist, which can be easily and quickly followed in a crisis.

Educators tend to do this for such traditional safety issues as fire emergencies, natural disasters, environmental situations, death or serious illnesses, and similar concerns. Nevertheless, security-related issues are often missing from this important area of planning. Although schools have made significant improvements in this area in the past 5 years, there is still plenty of room for more work.

Crisis preparedness guidelines should, at a minimum, address the following security-related issues:

- Abductions, including kidnapping and removal of students by noncustodial parents
- Altercations or riots, such as gang, racial or other large-scale student disruptions or conflicts
- Bomb threats and suspicious device management
- Gunfire, in school and on school grounds
- Hostage situations, including on school buses
- Trespassers and suspicious persons in school or on school property, including on school buses
- Weapons possession, threats, and/or use
- Other violations of state law and local ordinances pertinent to school operations

Safety or other noncriminal issues also should be included in the crisis preparedness guidelines. Some of these events could occur because of criminal activity, but for the sake of organization, they have been included in this list.

- Accidents with massive injuries, either large-scale, within the school, or involving school buses
- Death, on or off school grounds, or serious illness involving a student, staff member, or another significant individual associated with the school

- Environmental, such as a chemical spill or toxic exposure
- Fire or explosion (criminally intentioned or an accident)
- Gas leak, power or water outage, or other operational service disruption
- Student protests or demonstrations
- Weather and natural disasters

Educators may prefer to have safety and noncriminal guidelines in a separate section adjacent to the security or criminal threats or they may wish to have one guideline reference with all issues in alphabetical order for quick reference. The most important aspect of the format is that it is accessible, practical, and usable by any staff member during a highly emotional crisis period.

Crisis preparedness guideline development is, in itself, worthy of an entire book. Although many suggestions can be made on this subject, the reality is that crisis preparedness guidelines must be tailored to the individual district and to the individual schools. Besides going through the "What if?" questions with the previously mentioned and other issues, crisis teams should do the following:

1. *Define and list characteristics and levels of a crisis for the team's district, school, or both.* What is a crisis for one is not always a crisis for others.

2. *Establish roles and responsibilities of crisis team members, backup members and nonmembers.* Do not assume that all crisis team members will be at work or available at the time of the crisis. Make sure crisis team members include law enforcement and emergency service personnel who may be involved in an emergency response to your schools. When developing guidelines also be sure to include such support staff as counselors, psychologists, media liaison staff, nurses, custodians, secretaries, transportation personnel, and others who play critical roles in crisis management.

3. *Identify communications systems and emergency codes.* Remember to keep codes simple because many people do not think clearly at the time of a crisis.

4. *Locate floor plans and make them available prior to a crisis.*

5. *Determine who will handle media, parents, and other inquiries and notifications at the time of a crisis.* Also determine where they will be handled and how.

6. *Identify resource people, information, materials and related things that will be needed to support crisis response and management.* Make sure all of these are accessible or information on reaching them will be accessible at the time of the crisis.

Again, these are basic starting points. The process is complex and tedious. Nevertheless, experience shows that whereas there are no guarantees for preventing crises, these can be better managed through advance preparation and discussion.

One simple example illustrates the importance of the crisis preparedness planning process. In a crisis training session for educators and law enforcement in a midwestern state, the group was asked to list the basic steps they would take in a hostage situation. Working at different tables, one group of educators stated unquestionably that it would evacuate all classrooms not near the hostage situation. Meanwhile, another group, which had a law enforcement representative, stated without hesitation that it would contain all classrooms until inspection and an "all-clear" or other directions were received from law enforcement.

In short, had these individuals not participated in a crisis preparedness planning session, student and staff lives may have been placed in greater danger if an actual hostage situation had occurred than they would be without any advance planning. By talking out the "What if?" questions prior to a crisis, different perspectives were discussed and a new understanding was developed of how others would respond to this particular crisis situation. The resulting set of guidelines reduced the risks of additional injuries that could have occurred because of inadequate preparation.

Some basic assessment questions related to crisis preparedness include these:

1. Have the basic criminal or security threats and noncriminal threats been put to the "What if?" test?

2. Has the process involved the necessary representatives from within and outside the school or school system?

3. Has the product—that is, the crisis guidelines document—been deemed accessible, practical, and usable?

4. Have all school personnel been trained on and provided with copies of the crisis guidelines?

5. Have simulations or mock crisis exercises been conducted to test the guidelines and the response of school and other officials?

In other words, is the crisis preparedness document a living tool or a dust collector prepared simply for the sake of having guidelines?

Personnel and Internal Security

In addition to not reporting student crimes, school systems are equally, if not more, notorious for handling employee misconduct "internally." Many examples exist in which school systems have refused to prosecute employees who commit such crimes as improper relationships with students, thefts, embezzlement, and more. In lieu of prosecution, employee misconduct is frequently handled with administrative disciplinary action (similar to some student criminal offenses), and in more serious offenses, acceptance of a forced "resignation" from the employee.

Forced resignations may include an agreement that the district will not include any record of the offense in the employee's personnel file. It might also include an agreement that the district will not provide negative information when a prospective employer inquires about the employee for a position elsewhere. The result is that the problem employee is transferred to another agency, usually a different school system.

School systems also have a history of conducting limited background checks on potential employees. Although laws have been enacted in many states that require criminal history checks of new employees for school districts, many problems still exist regarding school hiring practices as they relate to background checks. These include the following:

1. As noted, the absence of a criminal history does not necessarily indicate the absence of past criminal conduct, even when such misconduct had been detected and confirmed. Criminal history checks are limited in that they show only those instances of arrests, prosecutions, and/or convictions. Considering the traditional practices of school systems in handling internal matters, it is relatively safe to say that a significant number of employee criminal offenses have gone unrecorded.

2. State laws, district policies, or both, regarding criminal history checks, may be limited to such classifications of employees as teachers, counselors, or administrative personnel. Volunteers, uncertified support employees, or such contract personnel as school photographers, building tradespeople, or "outsourced" school service providers, may never even receive this basic check.

3. Criminal history checks may be limited to a particular local, county, or state jurisdiction. Depending on the scope of the criminal history check, an applicant could potentially have a record in a neighboring county that will never show up on the records check.

4. Even if the criminal records are checked for all new applicants, a bigger problem exists regarding employees hired prior to the start of this type of record check. In a number of instances, employees have been convicted of criminal offenses outside the workplace and the school system was never notified. The result: The employee continues working with children while he or she has a criminal record.

All school systems should have a policy mandating employees to notify the employer when they are arrested or convicted of any crime, misdemeanor, or felony. This is still not enough because, unfortunately, many people will not notify the employer in the hope that the incident will never be discovered. For that reason, school systems should be required to perform periodic criminal history update checks on individuals during their periods of employment.

Although this may sound harsh, those questioning such a practice should ask themselves if they want a convicted criminal to supervise and serve as a role model for their children. Individuals who accept positions of working with children should expect such actions to be a reality of the times. If they do nothing wrong, they should not have to worry about being checked.

5. Few districts conduct what security professionals would call a true background check. Some may go as far as to send letters to former employers and references listed on the applications. Few actually have enough staff to go out in the field to talk with people and dig deep for character references and concrete verification of application information. Unfortunately, some readily accept what is on the application or résumé and never check anything except the required criminal history.

School districts should have a standard procedure for investigating and documenting alleged employee misconduct. Statements should be taken from all victims, witnesses, and suspects. Criminal offenses should be immediately reported to the police once they are detected. As with students, criminal offenders should be prosecuted and handled administratively, not simply one or the other.

Another aspect of internal security includes the security of information. Student files, personnel records, computerized information, and other district files and records are frequently left open and accessible to anyone who wants to gain access. Although certain records are public information, school systems need to take a close look at the security procedures for maintaining the integrity of information.

Computer hackers, reporters, and others with an interest in obtaining certain information find schools easy targets. Schools have always been "user-friendly" and school employees find it extremely difficult to challenge strangers or question individuals even when, at heart, they feel uncomfortable. Open doors, unchallenged strangers, unlocked file cabinets, and computer systems with no security measures provide unauthorized information seekers with perfect targets. In fact, a reporter once noted that if she wanted to know anything or to see what was new, she simply walked through and looked on the desks of central office administrators when they were away. She would always find something!

When assessing this area of school security, a close look should be taken at district hiring practices and background check procedures. Questions should include the following:

- Are background checks really conducted?
- Does the district require criminal history checks?
- What are the limitations of such checks?
- Are all employees checked or just certain classifications of employees?
- Does the district have a policy requiring employees to report arrests or convictions during their term of employment?
- Is there a standard process in place for investigating and documenting employee misconduct?
- Are employee criminal offenses prosecuted or simply "transferred" to another employer through forced resignations?
- Does the school system use appropriate information security measures?

Security assessments should not be an adversarial process in which the assessors are treated as though they are enemy spies. When assessing personnel and internal security, however, security professionals often find that this is the case. The assessment purpose is to identify strengths and weaknesses. School officials need to view this component with as much seriousness as the others. It could save a great deal of embarrassment and legal liability down the road.

Physical Security

The majority of elementary and secondary schools in the United States were not designed with security in mind. In fact, many of them are unintentionally designed for disaster, in terms of professional security standards. Poor visibility, inadequate communications, excessive access points, varying levels of lighting, limited intrusion detection systems, nonexistent key control, inconsistent or inaccurate inventory control, and inoperable or nonexistent locks characterize the state of security in many of these schools.

Clearly, this section alone could easily be developed into a book. In many cases, this component of the final report on a professional security assessment actually could be close to the size of a book. It is for this reason that many of the individuals "selling" security assessments to school districts today focus largely, if not solely, on the physical security component.

The following sections identify some key physical security areas and illustrate some practical issues to be considered in the school security assessment.

Access Control

Most schools have far too many access points. Not only do they have many doors, but in many districts, most of these doors are left unlocked and accessible from the outside. This problem could be corrected rather easily by using panic bars that secure the door from the outside but will facilitate egress from inside the building in the event of such an emergency as a fire.

School officials often mistake this type of reduction in access points as a fire hazard. Chaining doors from the inside creates a fire hazard. Proper use of panic bars on doors creates no fire hazard if occupants can leave the building in an emergency.

The reality is that access control is more an issue of convenience than anything else. Whereas some say that parents or other visitors will complain about having all doors secured from the outside except one designated entrance, it is often more an inconvenience for staff. If school officials educate parents, staff, students, and visitors of the necessity for access control, resistance should eventually decrease.

Some schools have secured all doors from the outside and established one designated entrance point. This designated entrance door is also secured from the outside and access is controlled by electronic buzzer, frequently integrated with video surveillance, speaker systems, or both. This works particularly well at the elementary level but can be less effective at larger schools with a significant amount of pedestrian traffic.

One elementary school principal felt that she had the most secure building in the district. All doors were secured from the outside and the designated entrance had a buzzer system. What the principal failed to consider was that more than half of the main entrance was made of glass, creating an easy target for those choosing to simply knock out the glass and open the door from the inside, particularly at night. Fortunately, a security assessment at that school resulted in a change in the type of door.

Open windows accessible from ground level and unsecured roof hatches also present access control problems. Many schools have adjacent playgrounds where children and youths spend many evenings and late nights. It is not uncommon for them to climb onto the roof of the building or crawl inside through an open window. It is also not uncommon for vandalism and other damage to follow.

Different school designs present different access problems. A large number of districts have such portable classrooms as trailers or single-story houses that can be moved around on school grounds or from school to school. Whereas portable classrooms meet overcrowding needs of the district, they also create a significant security concern about unlocked doors, no communications link to the main building, and the need to have students walking from portables to main buildings during the school day.

One school district had a very serious access problem related to student rest rooms at several elementary and middle school buildings. Many student rest rooms were scattered throughout the campus and were only accessible from the outside of the building. This meant that students had to exit their classrooms and enter rest rooms from the outside of the building. At the time of a security assessment, these rest rooms were unlocked and accessible to anyone who gained access to school grounds.

Obviously, this presented a serious security risk because trespassers, child molesters, kidnappers, or just about any other person wanting to hide inside the rest rooms could do so. Of course, the security assessment report included strong recommendations related to locking the rest room doors and having students escorted by adults. The ideal recommendation, although costly, was to have these rest rooms relocated and accessible from inside the building.

Persistent individuals will likely gain access to the school if they really want to do so. Doors will be left partially open by legitimate users, and in larger schools, students will inevitably open doors for individuals coming in. Still, an aggressive effort to control access points should be maintained and signs should be posted on all doors directing visitors to the main office, along with signs posted throughout the building indicating the actual location of the main office.

Regardless of the number of secured doors or signs, school staff must assertively challenge visitors and strangers observed in their building. Security assessments of various schools have found staff to be extremely friendly and blatantly indifferent to the presence of strangers in their school. Staff awareness programs must be implemented in concert with other access control measures.

Basic visitor control should include the following steps:

1. Limit access points
2. Post signs, directions, and/or floor plans
3. Greet, question, identify, and log visitors
4. Provide identification badges and escorts for visitors
5. Sign out visitors in a logbook when they leave
6. Train staff to challenge visitors and students to report strangers

These and other such measures as maintaining closed campuses at student lunchtime, should be included in this part of the security assessment process.

Communications

Many schools have antiquated communication systems, if any at all. Basic questions to be asked in the assessment of this area include:

1. Can teachers contact the office through in-house phones or by use of a panic button in each classroom?
2. Is there a public address system that can be used to broadcast emergency messages through the school? It is also helpful to have two-way public address systems by which broadcasts can be made and individual rooms can be monitored on the same system.
3. Does the school have two-way portable walkie-talkie or radio units for use in routine and emergency situations?
4. Can pay phones be removed from the hallways and school grounds, to reduce loitering, rumor control, false 911 calls, and related misuse?

School officials also may want to consider purchasing a cellular phone for use in crisis situations when mobility is needed or when regular phone systems are down.

Some progressive districts have been able to get the business community to donate cellular services for such purposes.

Identification Systems

School officials have debated the value of ID cards at the secondary school level for years and they still appear to have no conclusive position on whether the benefits outweigh the costs.

Adult ID cards are helpful in identifying central office staff, employees from other schools, contract employees, substitute staff, and other individuals not normally assigned to a particular school. Student identification cards are also helpful in controlling school bus riders and identifying trespassers in buildings, but they are not foolproof. Adult and student identification systems require regular and consistent enforcement, with clear consequences and costs for those who fail to wear the cards.

Yes, wear them. What good is an identification card if it is tucked away in a wallet or pocket? The time consumed in repeatedly requesting identification cards, and replacing them, seems to be a major factor in the demise of most well-intentioned identification programs. Costs of implementing and maintaining such programs is another strong factor.

Schools with a large staff and student body are also likely to run into parking problems. A vehicle identification program for all cars parked on school property should be maintained. Cars should be registered with security personnel, the main office, or both, with vehicle description, license number, and related identification information for staff and student vehicles. Here again, information security is important to keep staff identification information out of the hands of students.

Regardless of whether student and staff identification systems are in place, visitor identification should be mandatory in all schools. In addition to the recommendations related to access control, visitors should be issued a clearly visible identification tag to be worn at all times that they are on school premises. Relatively inexpensive time-lapse visitor badges are now available from security product vendors that change colors or are otherwise altered after a predetermined time or following exposure to outside light. These disposable badges help maintain the integrity of the visitor identification program without creating excessive worries about "walk away" badges.

The bottom line for identification systems is simple: If you are going to do it, do it consistently and properly. Operational and enforcement logistics should be thoroughly discussed before seriously taking steps to implement such programs.

Intrusion Detection Systems

Intrusion detection systems, or alarms, vary from district to district and even from school to school. Generally, school districts have antiquated, fragmented, and/or nonexistent intrusion detection systems. Poor maintenance, irregular inspections, employee abuse of systems, and related factors contribute to their reduced effectiveness.

This area should receive increased attention, particularly when considering the infusion of high-tech computers and other technology into classrooms today. It is not surprising to find schools with several million dollars worth of computer technology, particularly at the high school or magnet school levels. It is surprising to find adequate security systems associated with this equipment and their storage areas.

Are systems antiquated or adequate? Are the systems fragmented or do multiple systems (and even multiple alarm companies) cover the same school, causing duplication, confusion, or ineffective coverage? Security assessments should address these and other questions related to intrusion detection systems.

It may be appropriate to have a technical consultant with expertise in this specific area assist with the assessment. Larger districts with internal security departments may find it valuable to have a dedicated staff member(s) to deal solely with intrusion detection systems and related alarms. The importance of maintaining alarm systems, making the appropriate system adjustments when high-value items are moved, and planning for future needs cannot be overstated.

Inventory Control

Inventory control is sorely lacking in most school systems. The larger the district, the greater the chance that this is the case. Yet thousands, and in many districts millions, of dollars in equipment are floating around school systems and out the doors of school systems, with no accountability.

Identification mechanisms should be permanently affixed onto or engraved in the property, along with a clear identification of the school district to which it belongs. Most districts set a dollar limit on items requiring inventory tags or labels. Unfortunately, some districts set an exceptionally high limit on the dollar amount to avoid difficulties in finding items at the time of an audit. If it is too difficult to find $500 worth of video equipment that may be missing at audit time, districts simply set a limit for labeled items at more than $500 so that everything under that amount will not have to be tracked down.

Again, technology has helped address security concerns. Bar codes offer a new tool for inventory control. Outside agencies are available to contract with schools to inventory all property. Although some school officials argue that it costs too much to perform such a service, would it not cost more to replace stolen or lost property?

Key and Lock Control

Most schools have terrible key control. In some schools, keys that have been duplicated, lost, or stolen are often more accessible to students than staff. A high school in one city actually had its own key duplication machine in an assistant principal's office with boxes of blank keys openly available!

Many security professionals are amazed by how many classroom doors have no locks. This presents quite a problem in securing classrooms during teacher free periods and overnight. It presents a greater problem in crisis planning if a "lockdown" is needed to prevent intruders from entering individual classrooms.

The user-friendly mentality can create other problems, even when all doors have locks. Crime prevention awareness must be ingrained in the school culture to make locking cabinets and doors routine behavior. Numerous incidents have illustrated the benefits of such practices, including several fires set in custodial closets that might have been prevented had the doors been locked.

Locks and other security devices need to be purchased for computer and other high-tech equipment placed in schools today. It should not be surprising to see a shift in after-hour entry suspects from juveniles to young adults, considering the amount of equipment in many schools today. Traditionally, juveniles broke into schools to vandalize property. Expect older thieves to target schools in upcoming years for expensive equipment that they can easily fence on the streets, particularly in the absence of inventory control records, police reports, or both, to identify missing items accurately.

Assessments should include a review of key control, presence and use of locks, and related issues.

Perimeter and Outside Security

Many schools have poorly defined perimeters, transition markers, or barriers from street traffic. Playground equipment, poles, and other structures often provide easy access to fire escapes, roofs, and other potential entry points. Trees, shrubs, and related greenery frequently offer perfect concealment for juvenile parties, vandalism, or entry into schools at night.

Inspections of perimeter and outside security should be conducted during the school day and at night. This is especially true for buildings where night school programs are conducted. Schools have as much responsibility for security at night as they do during the day.

In earlier years, afterschool problems could be easily detected by school personnel working late evenings and nights for special events. Recent budget cuts and the elimination of afterschool programs, especially after dark, have resulted in many staff members leaving school immediately. Those who do work late usually have one goal when leaving the building, to get home quickly and safely! They are not likely to hang around to assess security.

Protective Lighting

Protective lighting, which used to be a simple issue, has been increasingly debated over recent years. Some advocates of a "lights out" policy unquestionably hold that this is the only way to go. They argue that by turning out all lights and requiring school neighbors and others in the area to report any signs of light to police, thieves will be caught much faster because they need light to do their dirty work.

Many security professionals still question this practice. The lights-out philosophy is frequently supported and advocated more from an energy (and dollar) conservation perspective than from a professional security perspective. Whereas it may work in some areas, particularly in rural or smaller suburban communities, security professionals working with larger, urban districts question whether lights-out is the best approach.

Most such lights as individual classroom lights, inside a school, should be turned off. The efficiency and logic of having a school completely lit up are questionable. Nevertheless, good lighting outside the building deters the amateur vandal or burglar who might otherwise commit an offense under the protection of darkness. It is logical to follow lights-out on the inside and "lights-on" on the outside as a general recommendation, recognizing that schools and districts are unique and may require individualized recommendations.

Bigger lighting problems exist in many schools with timer adjustments, inadequate maintenance, and infrequent inspections of lighting conditions. Some school lots and grounds have been found to have timers that turn on the lights during the day and off at dark! Security assessments have also turned up reports of burned-out or damaged lights that have gone unrepaired for months prior to the inspection, even though the facility had been used on a daily basis.

Like other physical security issues, lighting generally requires financial commitments. This includes costs associated with repairs, replacement, and labor. Costs, however, should not automatically disqualify corrective action. It is better to pay smaller amounts for prevention than larger amounts for damage awards in court.

Signage

Most schools make poor use of signs outside and inside schools. Outside signs should include notices prohibiting trespassing, identifying drug-free and weapon-free zones, providing directions to visitors, and identifying specific entrances by number, letter, or both. Signs inside the school should include clear directions to the office and identification of different wings, program areas, or facilities.

One of the most disturbing practices is the posting of signs directing visitors to report to the main office; yet there are no signs or indicators of where the main office is located! Some schools have posted signs throughout the building pointing to the main office or nearest administrative office. Others have posted floor plans near each entrance so visitors have a map to follow in locating the appropriate office.

One high school, following a recommendation in a security assessment, posted improved signs outside the school to identify each entrance by letters and numbers and posted directional signs and floor plans inside the building near each entrance. The benefits for this particular school were quickly observed during the upcoming months owing to the large size of the campus. In one situation, the response to an administrator's call to 911 for an ambulance and police was quickly expedited. The caller simply asked that the ambulance driver and the police be sent to "Door C3 and follow the blue 'Office' sign," rather than giving 3 or 4 minutes of detailed directions that could easily be confused at a time of crisis.

Other Issues

This section highlights some key basic issues in physical security. It is not presented as an exhaustive list. Such issues as preventing crime through design, especially when building new schools, and the many other more detailed issues related to physical security should be pursued by an experienced security professional.

The physical security component of the security assessment can be very detailed and lengthy. It clearly illustrates the importance of having an assessment performed by a school security professional instead of a nonsecurity official. Whereas checklists can be used to point out many more details in the different categories, nothing is better than a personal inspection by an experienced security professional to identify unique problems or potential problems at each school.

Education and Training

Policies, procedures, staffing, crisis guidelines, and other security measures will have minimum influence if school officials fail to provide adequate training on security and crime prevention issues. Policy makers, administrators, teachers, support staff, students, parents, law enforcement, and other key stakeholders should be trained on a regular basis. Topics should include updates on such threats as gangs, drugs, weapons, criminal offenses, and security procedures.

The security assessment should determine whether training is provided, and if so, whether it is provided for the appropriate individuals. Training and education programs also may be assessed to determine the relevance and content appropriateness.

Community Coordination

School relationships with law enforcement, criminal justice, social service and other youth service providers also should be reviewed in the security assessment. Efforts should be made to determine if school officials have true relationships or just surface-level contacts and if the relationships are with the proper individuals. Rumor control mechanisms, response protocols, and other formal and informal agreements should be reviewed.

Linking Security With
Intervention and Prevention

Security personnel and law enforcement are often improperly labeled as too punitive and insensitive to intervention and prevention needs. Security officials are quick to point out, however, that secure environments must exist for prevention and intervention programs to be effective. Security assessments should include a look at whether there are internal linkages of security programs with intervention and prevention programs.

This is not to say that security officials have to personally supervise or operate intervention and prevention programs, although many are actively involved in such projects in addition to their traditional security duties. It does mean, however, that security managers should meet regularly and work closely with intervention and prevention staff to head off future problems. Effective school security personnel will work with such administrators as those in pupil services to improve communications and strategies because discipline and security often overlap. They also should work with intervention and curriculum personnel to help identify the issues and trends observed in security department data and field work so that these officials can develop realistic prevention and intervention programs on the basis of what is actually going on at the front lines.

6

Popular Security Strategies and Issues

W hat about metal detectors? What about drug-sniffing dogs? What about uniforms?

Questions such as these grow in number at every "safe schools" conference. Unfortunately, research is limited and professional opinions on many of these subjects are often anecdotal. Some common themes and considerations often overlooked by educators and even security personnel are highlighted below.

Bomb Threats and Suspicious Devices

Bomb threats to schools usually have been motivated by hopes of early school dismissal, instructional interruptions, and in some cases, anger or revenge directed toward school staff. School officials face a new challenge, however, with increasing domestic terrorism threats, heightened public attention to bomb scares, and easy access on the Internet to formulas for making homemade explosive devices. Bomb threats have been replaced with actual devices in school buildings and on school grounds.

Administrators should take these basic steps to properly manage bomb threats and suspicious devices.

1. Inform staff that all bomb threats and suspicious devices must be treated as if they are real. The shifting trend from "hoax" incidents to the "real thing" must be quickly recognized and treated seriously.

2. Coordinate with law enforcement bomb specialists in developing specific procedures for handling threats and devices before an incident occurs. Although there are some common issues in most response plans, local concerns and protocol must be adapted to individual school and district guidelines.

3. Assess physical security issues when developing bomb guidelines.

4. Incorporate these basic components into your guidelines:

   a. Bomb threat telephone call checklists and procedures

   b. Procedures and roles of notifiers for informing law enforcement and other staff of a threat, suspicious device, or both

   c. Guidelines for conducting visual search inspections of common areas and individual rooms

   d. Procedures for securing an area where a suspicious device is located

   e. Evacuation plans for the building and grounds

   f. Contingency plans for an actual explosion incident

5. Train all staff, including secretaries, custodians, and support staff, on bomb threat management procedures. Although secretaries often receive the threat calls and custodians may be the first to find suspicious packages, they are often not included in staff development training sessions. Practical exercises and search drills should be included in the training.

Law enforcement bomb specialists are the best resource for school administrators to develop specific guidelines. Most police departments either have specialists on staff or access to specialists in other departments. Because they will be the individuals responding to an actual bomb-related incident at your school, including them in front end planning is essential.

Computer Security Measures

How will your school handle bomb and death threats sent by electronic mail? How can you protect your school computer records, schedules, and employee payroll data from being changed by hackers? Can your students produce counterfeit money using school computers, scanners, and printers?

Schools are adding new computers and technology to classrooms daily across the United States. One of the biggest challenges is not for the children and youths but for the adults. How can adults adapt to the new technology and keep one step ahead of the students or other hackers to ensure that it is not abused?

Over the past year, very informal surveys on this issue have been made on seminar attendees at schools, including administrators, teachers, and students. Staff and students were asked to raise their hands if they were on the Internet and if they had electronic mail accounts. Inevitably, many more students than adults raised their hands. Sometimes three or four more times the number of students are hooked into current technology than the adults supervising them!

School officials need to address not only physical security issues related to computers and other equipment but also the potential for abuse of services. Policies and procedures regarding abuse or misuse of school equipment, computer systems and networks, and the Internet should be implemented and modified as technology advances are brought into the schools. Staff should be fully trained in the use of all new technology used by students. Districts should provide training and resources for keeping their personnel up with the times. Administrators and staff can and should request such training.

Drug-Sniffing Dogs

One principal was overheard saying, "I bring drug dogs into my school all the time." When asked how often they check the lockers, the principal replied, "Oh, I don't let them check the lockers. I just bring them into an assembly to scare the kids!" The other principal responded, "You're so progressive. I only bring them in at night when nobody else is around."

Sad to say, this was not a joke. A number of administrators who bring drug dogs into the school only do so when students and staff are not in the building or for "show-and-tell" purposes in assemblies. When it comes to actually having the dogs perform, many principals back off.

A great deal of the fear of using drug dogs can be attributed to the political and image issues discussed in Chapter 2. Other misconceptions may center on a fear that the dogs will somehow hurt the students. Many simply fear what the dogs may actually find.

Recommendations and considerations about the use of drug-sniffing dogs include the following:

Recognize in advance that serious drug dealers will likely have their "products" concealed on their person, where the dogs cannot check anyway. Some traces of drugs stored in lockers at some point may be detected, even if the contraband is not there at the time of the search. Still, the chances are that the use of drug-sniffing dogs will not culminate in massive arrests with bulk drug confiscations.

If you are going to do it, do it right! Drug dogs largely serve as a deterrent. To bring them in at night when nobody is in the building is not a deterrent. Not only is no one present to be deterred, but the chances are also good that students will not leave drugs in lockers overnight.

Likewise, bringing dogs in for an assembly is a good idea if principals plan to follow through with actual inspections during the school year. Dog demonstrations will show students what they can expect and the overall effectiveness of the dog in detecting drugs. This strategy is a deterrent. To hope that this alone will "scare" the students into not bringing drugs, without actually following up with some real enforcement of the inspection procedure is, at best, an administrator's fantasy.

Do not issue advance warnings about a specific inspection. This includes not only keeping it a secret from students but also from staff. Everyone knows the effectiveness of the lounge grapevine. If one staff member knows, the chances are that all staff members and a good number of students will know.

This does not mean that notice of a potential dog inspection should not be given at the beginning of the year. District policies and handbooks should include notice that the school is subject to such an inspection, without prior warning, at any time during the school year. Parents also should be notified of this potential. Nobody, however, should be notified of a specific inspection by a public address announcement that, "Tomorrow we will have a drug dog search at 9:00 A.M." Believe it or not, this happens!

In fact, one suburban school district leader reportedly decided that she was going to have "zero tolerance" with drugs in her high schools. After 2 years of ignoring pressure from local law enforcement officials to bring drug-sniffing dogs into her secondary schools, the superintendent coordinated a simultaneous sweep of all three public high schools shortly before the end of the school year. It was later learned by the police that 2 weeks prior to the sweep, with only several weeks left in the entire school year, school administrators had students carry home letters to parents announcing that drug sweeps would be taking place before the end of the school year. It was not surprising that the sweeps were not productive!

Do not believe that drugs are not present nor available simply because a search comes up empty. As previously noted, the majority of "successful" drug dealers will have their product on their person or close at hand. It is ludicrous to believe that no "hits" on all of the lockers equals a drug-free school!

Do not be embarrassed or apologetic if drugs are found. The purposes of the inspection are to find drugs and to send a deterrent message. If drugs are found and the perpetrators face consequences, the inspection has served its purposes.

Most parents, students, and community members will support such initiatives if they are properly educated on the subject and the process is done professionally. Problems tend to arise when the reasons for such actions are not made clear in advance and when such programs are implemented haphazardly.

Hotlines

A number of schools find success with security-related hotlines either at the building, district levels, or both. Some hotlines simply involve a dedicated line with an answering machine. Others are more elaborate, such as having a tie-in with local "crime stoppers" programs or other financial incentives.

A hotline is only as effective as the follow-up on tips and the publicity of its existence. Notices of hotlines should be included in public-address announcements, student handbooks, posters throughout the schools, parent and community newsletters, and advertisements through the media. Many administrators find that student callers are less interested in rewards than they are in effective follow-through to resolve their safety concerns.

One school resource officer took the hotline concept a step further. Knowing that his students were active with current technology, he implemented a tip-line by computer electronic mail. He advertised his screen name and included it on his business cards. Students sent confidential electronic mail tips about rumors of fights and other security-related information.

Not only did he find this high-tech hotline a success with school-related tips, but he also was able to prevent a student suicide, thanks to his computer availability after school. The officer was informed by a student in a computer chat room that another student had consumed a large number of pills in a suicide attempt while a group of youths was at her home. The officer immediately sent police and medical assistance to the student's home, besides responding himself. The report was accurate, and fortunately, the suicide attempt was thwarted.

This illustrates not only the importance of an anonymous hotline but also the importance of using such student interests as technology to address educational and safety issues.

Lockers and Bookbags

Some schools feel forced to more drastic actions to improve safety. These include elimination of lockers and bookbags. Others have modified the approach by requiring "see-through" bookbags in which the contents are clearly visible.

Elimination of lockers and bookbags sounds great, but there are many implications. It usually means that districts provide one set of books for the classroom and another set for students to take home. In many districts, this is not financially possible.

See-through bookbags serve as an extra tool for security. Of course, this is not a panacea. Students who want to carry weapons or other contraband can simply conceal them on their person or within something else in the bookbag.

Proper procedures related to student searches provide an alternative for those school officials unable to implement locker and bookbag elimination. Students should be given prior notice that they are subject to search if administrators have a reasonable suspicion that they violated school rules or the laws. They also should be advised, in advance, that lockers are the property of the school, and as such, they are subject to search at any given time during the school year.

Metal Detectors, Cameras, and Other Equipment

School officials who face a high-profile incident or crisis, frequently turn to security-related equipment as a "quick fix" to illustrate to staff, students, parents, and the community that they are taking action to deal with security concerns. Unfortunately, many equipment-related measures are undertaken without full consideration of the implications and operational issues associated with such ventures. Equipment should be a supplement to, not a substitute for, professional security personnel, policies, procedures, and programs.

Educators must recognize the limitations of metal detectors. They are not a total solution for preventing weapons in school. Schools with metal detectors still have had incidents of guns, knives, and other weapons in school.

Students smuggle weapons through or around metal detectors. Some students have climbed into the building through windows or used other entrance points to avoid inspections conducted at the so-called single point of entry. Others have passed weapons through windows, under doors, or used other methods for getting them into the building.

This is not intended to say that metal detectors do not serve a deterrent purpose or that they are not effective in locating some weapons. Guns, knives, beepers, and other devices and paraphernalia have been found by metal detectors. Formal data and research are lacking nationally, however, to validate the exact effectiveness of such measures.

Anecdotal information suggests that administrators are more receptive to the random use of handheld metal detectors than to the use of stationary detectors. Random inspections of students boarding or exiting school buses, students taken from a random number of classrooms or periodic use at special events have reportedly kept students off guard about when they can expect to be checked. Keeping students off balance by the potential for inspection at any time seems to be critical in effectively using metal detectors.

Issues regarding notice are similar to those previously mentioned about drug-sniffing dogs, including, If you are going to do it, do it right! One school district canceled their metal detector inspections because they found "only" six weapons the previous year!! The questions are, How many more would have been brought to school without the inspections, and was "only" six an acceptable number of guns?

Likewise, thought should be given to all of the issues prior to implementing surveillance camera equipment. Many times, cameras are purchased and installed because of the availability of funds or the need to meet a public relations crisis. Administrators must also consider underlying issues such as installing cameras where they will be most effective, determining who will monitor the cameras, and identifying funding sources for the necessary repairs and replacement of equipment.

Good common sense is especially important when setting up cameras. Cameras should not be placed in a location where there are such reasonable expectations of privacy as rest rooms or locker rooms. Although such locations may be priority areas in terms of security problems, other liability concerns will be equally high if an administrator chooses to place cameras in locations such as these.

Another issue frequently ignored is whether a reasonable expectation exists for a response to problems that occur in the view of surveillance cameras. If a student or staff member is attacked and beaten in front of a camera, does that person have a reasonable expectation that security or administrative personnel will respond to assist? Likewise, what are the implications of using "dummy cameras" in which there may be a dozen camera boxes, but only two functional cameras are rotated among the boxes?

Many schools have purchased camcorders for use by their security, administrative personnel, or both. These have come in quite handy for taping trespassers, fights, or other criminal or disruptive behavior. Not only does the tape provide a good record to support disciplinary and/or criminal action, it also serves as a nice tool for "disarming" parents when they start to tell officials how their lovely children would never do what they are accused of doing.

School officials should consult with their legal counsels, develop appropriate policies and procedures, and train their personnel before implementing metal detectors, surveillance cameras, or similar programs.

Personal Safety

During the past decade, educators have voiced a growing fear for their personal safety. Threats include potential injuries from dealing with angry parents or intervening in fights and conflicts. Educators are also concerned about their own use of force and how they can reduce their potential for victimization.

Handling Angry Parents

Educators historically have faced angry parents on a rather frequent basis. Nobody likes to see his or her child fail classes, be disciplined, or in some cases, be arrested and prosecuted. School crime and disciplinary incidents have increased the chances of educators facing angry confrontations.

Some basic steps that can be taken to reduce risks associated with dealing with angry parents include the following:

1. Schedule conferences in advance, whenever possible.
2. Establish procedures to ensure that parents do not disrupt classes or "ambush" teachers or other staff during regularly scheduled business that should not be interrupted.
3. Recognize the need for parents to "vent." Their frustration may stem from months or years of problems with their children. (So may yours!) Also recognize, however, the point at which you must "draw the line" when parents' venting turns to abuse. Make sure there is an agreement between staff and administrators, in general and in advance, of where that "line" is acceptable to both staff and principals. Nothing is worse than having a staff member draw the line, only to have an administrator reverse the decision and place the staff member in an even more confrontational position.

4. If a problem is anticipated, ask another staff member to join in a parent conference and/or notify someone else about when you enter and will complete the conference and that you may call on him or her for assistance if a problem occurs.

5. Do not meet in isolated areas or where there is no way available to communicate with other staff members.

6. Leave your conference room door slightly ajar, in case you need assistance. Also, consider establishing code words or statements with other nearby employees that indicate a problem exists and you need help. For example, one principal believed that the mother in his office had a gun in her purse. As she became loud, the principal's secretary entered the office to give him some papers. Then he said to her, "Mrs. Smith, please schedule that meeting we discussed for this afternoon." Although it seemed normal to the parent, the secretary's real name was Mrs. Jones. The phrase was a code to send for assistance.

7. Focus parent conferences on how their concerns can be resolved in the best interests of the child. In other words, talk about what action needs to be taken from that point, not just what happened yesterday.

These are a few simple considerations. It is not an exhaustive list. Common sense and good planning will help reduce risks and may identify many other helpful steps that can be taken to prevent problems.

Intervening Safely in Fights and Conflicts

Many staff injuries are not received in student versus staff confrontations, but instead, occur when staff members break up fights or conflicts between two or more students. Many staff members subsequently may hesitate to break up student fights and conflicts, but their total inaction contributes to a likely increase in security risks. Unfortunately, students fight at school because they know that someone will usually break up the fight quickly.

Nobody can force staff members to physically intervene in a situation if they choose not to do so. Each staff member must assess in advance what his or her threshold is for physical intervention.

Regardless of whether they actually physically intervene, all staff members can play a role in assisting to restore order. This can include dispersing crowds, documenting observed behavior, and providing similar supportive actions.

School officials who do decide to physically intervene should remember some basic points.

1. Monitor for early warning signs of such conflicts as stare-downs, verbal exchanges, posturing, audience formation, and other clues that an altercation is about to ensue. Do not wait for the smoke, if you can put out the fire early on!
2. Remain calm and do not draw additional student attention to the incident.
3. Get assistance en route to the scene or as soon as possible.
4. Briefly assess the situation, including the participants, the audience, and your surroundings, before jumping into the middle of a crowd.
5. Watch hands as well as eyes. Remember that while someone may be looking in one direction, his or her hands could be going for a weapon!
6. Identify an escape route and do not be afraid to take it, if necessary. Heroes are for television, not school hallways. Let your common sense prevail in all situations.

These are just a few basic thoughts. Staff members should be trained on points similar to those above. Nevertheless, it is not advisable to try to teach your staff a full form of martial arts in one 20-minute staff meeting! It is unrealistic to attempt to instruct staff members on how to disarm students in such a short time, and it often creates a false sense of security.

Reducing Staff Victimization

School officials often lay the groundwork for reducing staff victimization far ahead of an actual confrontation. Officials are often helped to deal more effectively with students in a state of alarm by building positive relationships with them prior to a crisis. Officials who have good relationships with many students will have a good reputation among the student body as a whole. This also can be potentially helpful in dealing with others who may not actually have had contact with the staff member before an incident.

Educators, as well as security or police personnel, must strike the delicate balance of being firm, fair, and consistent in how they administer discipline and exert authority with children. Individuals who are perceived to be too weak or too hard are likely candidates for increased victimization. Effective staff will be firm, fair, consistent, organized, confident, supportive, and friendly but alert and cautious to a reasonable degree.

Use of Force

School districts should establish policies and procedures regarding employee use of force against students. This issue also should be addressed in staff meetings and training programs. Some general suggestions include:

1. Use of force by staff should be reasonable, necessary, and timely in the eyes of a prudent person.
2. Use of force should escalate only in response to the level of resistance and without malice by the staff member using the force.
3. Use of force should cease once compliance is achieved.
4. Use of force by staff in any incident should be documented and witness statements should be obtained immediately following the incident.

The potential always exists for liability. This potential will increase if severe injury occurs to students, when a staff member acts in anger, or when an action is disproportionate to the need. These issues and others, of course, are situational. The listed suggestions, and more important, advice from your district's legal counsel on sound school policies will help staff prepare to face such incidents.

Probation Officers in Schools

Some officials find it helpful to have court probation officers operate directly from their schools. An administrator from one large urban area claimed that more than one third of his entire high school study body was on probation at the same time! In that situation, it was easier to bring the services to the client, rather than the client to the services.

Benefits of such a program include:

1. Easier and more timely communication between the proba- tion officer and school officials (assuming that they form good relationships)
2. Earlier intervention with students in school conflicts that often lead to suspension and/or probation violations
3. Reinforcement of school rules and court orders that provides order, structure, and discipline for the youth

Difficulties that may arise include such travel logistics as required court appearances of the probation officer, access to a private office and operational equipment, and potential confidentiality issues that can arise if these issues are not planned for in advance. Still, it is a unique approach to providing collaborative services for at-risk and troubled youths.

Sex Offenses

There is a strong possibility that administrators will encounter an incident of "inappropriate touching" early in their administrative careers. Many administrators have difficulty in distinguishing be- tween what is "appropriate" and what is "inappropriate" touching. By waiting one school day to further investigate such cases, some administrators have received negative publicity, lawsuits, and threats of criminal charges by law enforcement officials.

Incidents of rape, sexual imposition, molestation, and related of- fenses can and do occur in school classrooms, hallways, buildings, and on school grounds. A review of state laws and local ordinances on sex-related crimes is a must for all school administrators and should be incorporated into annual administrator training programs. Policies, developed to be consistent with the laws, should be used to create clear guidelines on what, when, and how adminis- trators report sex offenses to law enforcers and parents.

Anytime a school official questions whether to call police on sex-related cases, the administrator should err on the side of caution and notify law enforcement authorities. Law enforcement officials have much more expertise than an average school administrator in handling such offenses. By involving law enforcement, administrators are operating in the best interests of the child and in their own best interests.

Student Searches

Most school officials are well-informed about their legal rights regarding when they may conduct a search if a student violates a law or the school rule. Few officials, however, have received training in how to actually perform an effective student search. All administrators and security personnel should receive training on the legal aspects of student searches and how to conduct a search.

Some basic tips on searching students include:

1. Personally escort the students to be searched to the office. Maintain visible contact with the students from the time they are retrieved from the classroom to the time they reach the predetermined destination. It would be prudent to have at least two staff members escort students, to provide extra support in monitoring students so they do not throw away any contraband, run, or attempt to assault or resist the escorting adults.

2. Always watch the students' hands. If a student is suspected of having a weapon or drugs, it is likely that he or she will try to "ditch" it if an opportunity arises. This can occur from the time the student is told to accompany a security or administrative official to the office up to and including the time when the student is actually in the office and searched. Never allow a student to follow behind a staff member where the student cannot be observed.

3. Before beginning the search, ask the students if they have anything in their possession, in a locker, or in anyone else's possession that violates the school rules or the law. If they hesitate, tactfully advise them that you have reasonable suspicion that they do, that you plan to conduct a search, and that it would save everyone time and

unnecessary embarrassment if students cooperate on the front end. As strange as it sounds, students often acknowledge that they do, with minimal hassles.

4. Ask students to remove such outer clothing as heavy jackets. It is difficult to effectively pat down a student wearing three layers of jackets!

5. Remember that concealment places are not limited to pockets. Determine, within legal and procedural parameters, how far you may search, but never assume that the absence of the item means that it is totally absent from the school.

6. Secure confiscated contraband and document the incident as soon as possible. If it is a criminal offense, notify police and maintain a clear chain of evidence until they arrive.

Administrators, teachers, and staff must remember that strip searches by school personnel are frowned on by the legal system, not to mention parents and the media! Unfortunately, cases continue to arise in which school officials conduct questionable searches, most often to look for money stolen from class fund-raising projects, the desks of teachers or students, and related areas. Generally, students will tell who took the money if timely and effective investigations are conducted. School officials must ask themselves, Is a strip search to find $30.00 worth losing my job, personal valuables, and public reputation?

Administrators should consult with local law enforcement, school security specialists, or both for training and establishing detailed procedures for conducting student searches.

Theft

Thefts of property belonging to the school district, its staff, and its students are fairly common. Perpetrators are not only students. Internal theft by school employees occurs in school buildings, office sites, warehouses, and other school facilities.

School systems often have inadequate inventory control and property transfer procedures, making it relatively easy for equipment and supplies to "walk" without someone noticing. Schools generally have inadequate or nonexistent key control, as reflected in one security officer's comment that "The students have more keys to this building than I do." Unfortunately, the trusting nature of educators also contributes to the problem, especially "opportunity thefts" created by individuals not securing valuable equipment, leaving purses and other properties accessible, failing to lock doors, and being overly friendly and not questioning unknown visitors.

What should administrators do to reduce thefts? Steps should include:

1. Establish key control procedures.
2. Institute and maintain an effective inventory control and property removal or transfer procedure.
3. Create an increased awareness between faculty and staff to reduce opportunity thefts. Encourage them to lock doors, secure keys and personal property, and question strangers observed in the school.
4. Report thefts of school and personal property to law enforcement. If suspects are identified, prosecute them and pursue restitution.
5. Establish an anonymous reporting system for students and staff, to provide tips on theft suspects and incidents.

Thefts are crimes and should be treated as such. If administrators place a strong emphasis on respect for school property and the property of individuals, and aggressively pursue those found stealing, thefts may decrease.

Transportation Security

School administrators, and certainly many bus drivers, feel that they are increasingly vulnerable to security threats while transporting students on school buses. Many districts cannot afford to hire adult monitors to supervise student behavior, leaving drivers to single-handedly manage traffic and student safety aboard the units. What can be done to improve security on buses?

Some practical strategies for managing transportation security include:

1. Install video surveillance cameras to monitor student behavior. Follow the guidelines previously referenced regarding notice and the legal concerns. Cameras serve as a deterrent to many students, and for those who are not deterred, the video serves as good evidence for administrators and parents to use to determine disciplinary, criminal, or both charges.

2. Train bus drivers to manage disruptive student behavior and current security threats such as gangs, drugs, and weapons. Drivers should be provided with training on personal safety, crisis preparedness, and related strategies to reduce risks.

3. Establish and maintain two-way radio communication equipment on all bus units, including communication methods for out-of-district field trips. First aid kits also should be placed on each bus.

4. Keep updated student rosters on all buses, including addresses, phone numbers, parent names, and related information for all students on all routes. Also, keep copies of medical authorization cards, if possible. This information is critical in case of serious accidents or other crises.

5. Include transportation staff in the development of crisis management guidelines. Buses are as vulnerable to a crisis as any other school site.

6. Encourage local law enforcement personnel to have their SWAT or emergency response units train aboard school buses. Hostage situations or other emergencies could take place on a school bus and it is possible that some police teams may not have been trained on school buses.

Discipline on buses should be a top priority for administrators. Regular communication and strong relationships between drivers and school administrators will go a long way toward creating a safe environment on school buses. If drivers are considered part of the school staff, students are likely to think twice before victimizing them than if the drivers have weak links to school authorities.

Trespassing

Former students, suspended or expelled students, truants, and strangers increasingly present problems for school administrators as trespassers on school property. Some basic suggestions for managing trespassing include:

1. Use effective access control procedures as previously mentioned.

2. Include trespassing as an offense in the student handbooks. Pursue trespassing cases with disciplinary and criminal action.

3. Communicate to students, early in the school year and periodically during the year, that they are not to have friends or relatives come to school grounds to meet with them before, during, or after school. Students who support and encourage trespassers should face disciplinary consequences.

4. Use a camcorder, camera, or similar device to record trespassers or nonstudents in the area of buses and school property at school dismissal. Often, these individuals are unknown to the staff of the school where they are trespassing, but they may be quickly identified by administrators of other schools in the area. Once trespassers or loiterers are identified, their home school administrators should pursue the appropriate disciplinary action.

Trespassing can lead to other incidents of violence and should be treated as a priority concern by school administrators, teachers, and staff.

Truancy

The United States is currently seeing a renewed interest in the issue of truancy. For many years, truancy has ranked on the low end of priorities of school and law enforcement. An increase in truant students' involvement in burglaries, auto thefts, trespassing for criminal purposes at schools other than their own, and other disruptive and illegal behavior has triggered new efforts to deal with truancy.

Police "sweeps" for truants have been conducted in many cities during the 1990s. In many communities, this process has been taken one step further. By collaborating with multiple agencies, communities are attempting to deal with the broader issues that motivate students to be truant. The purpose is to provide earlier identification and intervention for youths at risk for abuse, neglect, and delinquent behavior.

The Partnership for a Safer Cleveland, through its Youth Safety Leadership Committee, implemented a three-phase truancy sweep initiative early in 1996, following a similar operation in September of 1995. More than 400 truants, who had collectively missed a total of 14,452 days of school, were identified and processed by police, school, court, and social service representatives. Resulting intake data revealed that 29% of the students in the first sweep, 51% in the second sweep and 46% in the third sweep had active cases in court and family service agencies, allowing youth service agencies to identify students at risk and their families for early intervention and prevention services (L. M. Schmidt, personal communication, November 1996).

This unique collaboration includes participants from the city schools, public safety and police departments, prosecutor's office, county administration and human service offices, adult and juvenile courts, teachers union, and other nonprofit and private sector agencies. Police and school sweeps are immediately followed up with on-site assessments by court and social service representatives in an effort to better coordinate intervention and prevention services to children and their families. Project plans include development of an elementary prevention program for children ages 6 to 10 and their families.

Uniforms and Dress Codes

A growing number of schools are turning to uniforms and dress codes as an added tool in their safe and secure schools initiatives. As with the issues of equipment, drug-sniffing dogs, and other security strategies, research and professional opinions differ on the actual effect of this strategy on school security. On the front lines, however, there may be some agreement among school officials that student uniforms, dress codes, or both at least contribute to a more orderly educational environment.

A uniform, or standard form of dress, provides several positive contributions toward safer schools, including to:

1. Reduce student competition for status based on who has the most expensive clothing
2. Reduce (but not eliminate) methods for gang identification in school
3. Reduce opportunities for robberies of expensive clothing items often worn by students in school and to and from school
4. Help school staff more quickly identify trespassers and visitors who enter school buildings

Uniforms and dress codes are not a panacea for solving discipline and school security concerns. They do, however, provide another tool for addressing these issues.

School officials who consider uniforms should promote and encourage them but not necessarily mandate them without input from staff, parents, and students. Many schools voluntarily adopt uniforms with minimal resistance by involving students and parents on the front end of the process. Even parents who initially balked at the idea have changed their positions, once they discovered that clothing associated with school uniforms usually will be less expensive than other popular clothing. This saves parents money and arguments with their children over what to wear each day.

Vandalism

Some administrators ignore or downplay the seriousness of vandalism and other property crimes compared with such crimes against persons as assault and robbery. Although assaults and robberies cannot be treated lightly, the importance of dealing with "small" problems cannot be overlooked. If students perceive vandalism as minor offenses, they are likely to progress to more serious crimes once they get away with the others.

A few practical measures to reduce the risk of school vandalism include:

1. Distinguish vandalism from such crimes as burglaries and thefts. Whereas the latter generally involve unlawful entry, stealing property, or both, vandalism usually involves destroying or defacing property.

2. Document all vandalism incidents in internal incident reports and report crimes of vandalism to police. Vandalism costs are very high in many districts and cannot be written off as a part of doing business.

3. Identify high risk areas for vandalism as a part of your school security assessment. Ensure that staff lock windows, doors, and roof hatches to reduce entry points after hours.

4. Ensure that intrusion detection systems adequately cover school facilities.

5. Post "warning" signs that trespassers and vandals will be prosecuted. Seek restitution from prosecuted offenders.

6. Assess the layout and design of the school, inside and outside. Increase visibility of potential entry points by keeping trees, bushes, and shrubs cut and trimmed so they cannot conceal vandalism or cover unlawful entry points. Assess night lighting needs on a regular basis.

7. Have aggressive canvassing of the neighborhood by administrators and school security officials to encourage neighbors to monitor schools after-hours and to call police officials, school officials, or both when they observe vandalism, burglaries, trespassing, and other suspicious activity.

8. Repair or replace damaged property quickly. One broken window or graffiti-sprayed word will lead to a dozen more shortly thereafter, if they are not fixed.

9. Consider employing a mobile security patrol for nights and weekends in larger school districts with high vandalism rates.

Finally, school officials should create a school culture and climate of ownership and responsibility. Students and staff who feel connected to the school are less likely to vandalize property and take out their anger against the building.

Putting Together the Puzzle

Too often, school leaders look for the one-shot program or strategy that will enhance school security so they can move ahead with the many other tasks on their agenda. No one such program or strategy exists. Each school and each district must assess its own security posture and evaluate potential strategies based on the unique conditions prevailing at the particular point in time when security concerns are reviewed. They must then build on existing strategies to meet the new threats and demands.

7

Working Collaboratively With Students, Parents, Police, Community, and Media

You have distinguished myths from reality, pulled a representative group of stakeholders together and accepted some basic assumptions regarding school security. Now what? A collaborative focus is needed.

Ten Basic Collaboration Purposes

There are 10 basic purposes of addressing short-term and long-term needs through a balance of suppression, intervention, and prevention strategies. These 10 basic purposes or service areas provide a framework that not only addresses school-specific security needs but also the broader youth violence community issues that influence the safety of schools. "Programs should include a variety of coordinated services to youth, parents, schools, criminal justice personnel, residents, businesses, and community members" (Trump, 1996, p. 279). By working together, an effective collaborative community should provide the following services:

1. School-based intervention and investigation services for gang, drug, and other security incidents, concerns, and issues

2. Technical assistance in designing, refining, and implementing a comprehensive school safety and security program

3. Targeted police-suppression details and prosecution focused on problem areas and behaviors associated with gangs, drugs, and other juvenile crimes collectively identified by a multiagency group focused on these issues

4. Training and education programs on gangs, drugs, juvenile crime, school safety, and related issues for youths, school employees, criminal justice personnel, parents, community groups, and youth service professionals

5. Intelligence gathering, data collection and analysis, information sharing, and ongoing assessment of gang, drug, and juvenile crime trends, with accompanying response strategies, policies, programs, and procedures to minimize the growth and impact of these negative behaviors in their early stages

6. Facilitation of regular communication, information sharing, training, and joint cooperative efforts with neighboring communities, law enforcement agencies, and professional organizations to further networking, consistent programming, and information and resource sharing

7. Service as initiators or facilitators of new prevention and intervention programs by agencies and community organizations that further goals and objectives associated with gang and juvenile crime reduction

8. Service as a catalyst for the creation, modification, and implementation of legislation, strategies, programs, policies, and procedures to minimize the growth and impact of gangs, drugs, juvenile crime, and school safety threats

9. Service as a resource for technical assistance and current information for public officials, youth service providers, and others interested in gangs, drugs, juvenile crimes, and school safety

10. Collaborative efforts with local media to accurately inform the community about gang and juvenile crime problems and community responses without creating panic or overreaction (Trump, 1996, p. 279)

What's in It for Me?

People in the United States are driven by a "What's in it for me?" mentality. Whereas the broader concept, improving school security, may be conceptually appealing, members of different stakeholder groups need concrete contributions to meet the "What's in it for me?" question that drives them and their organizations. Some motivators for the different stakeholders involved in school security collaboratives might include:

1. *Businesses.* Threats to safe schools provide an unstable learning environment that contributes to truancy, increased dropouts, and increased crime. The immediate benefit to businesses may be that truants and other delinquents are off the streets and away from their businesses, resulting in a decrease in vandalism, robberies, and customer intimidation. The long-term benefit is a better educated, more productive workforce, and it is hoped, a more stable community with lower crime rates.

2. *Community residents and organizations.* These individuals and groups benefit in a manner similar to businesses. Not only do they share those specific interests, but they also benefit by increased property values through safer communities and better school systems.

3. *Media.* Media representatives benefit from participating in school security collaboratives by gaining an increased awareness of the issues they frequently cover in their news: juvenile crime, gangs, drugs, and school violence. They also obtain contacts and additional news stories of what their communities are doing to address these issues.

4. *Parents.* Parents want their children to be safe in school. They want an honest effort by school officials to deal with problems head-on and in a balanced, rational manner.

5. *Police and criminal justice personnel.* Law enforcement and criminal justice officials want safe schools and communities. They want crimes to be reported accurately, consistently, and in a timely manner. They do not want or need the additional work of school violence and crime to contend with, to justify their positions, or to maintain job security. School violence simply adds more headaches to an already burdened criminal justice system.

6. *Political and elected officials.* Board members, mayors, council members, and other elected officials want to get reelected! They do so by avoiding chronic problem issues, negative publicity, and related concerns. Safe schools are a political "win" for everyone if action backs the spoken words.

7. *Schools.* Educators want safe and secure settings where teachers can teach and children can learn. They want fairness in public expectations of their abilities to deal with the symptoms and the roots of youth and school violence. They expect public support and community ownership of school security and overall education issues.

8. *Social service and youth service providers.* Youth workers want to provide support in addressing the symptoms of underlying social and economic problems that contribute to juvenile crime and school violence. They, like law enforcement and criminal justice professionals, do not need heavier caseloads or more work to justify their existence. They expect a sincere opportunity to work with children and families, as well as education, criminal justice, and other systems, to provide their services.

9. *Students.* Very simply, they want to be safe in school and to and from school. They want input into problem identification and strategies for addressing these problems.

Because of individual stakeholder groups working together to ensure that their needs are met as a part of the safe school planning and action process, a greater commitment should be observable in the overall process.

Selling It to the Public

The media strike fear in many educators, particularly school administrators. Negative publicity can be the kiss of death to the career of a principal, central office administrator, or superintendent. How can you deal with the issues and the media?

Basic suggestions for dealing with the media include these:

1. Remember that the media will cover your story with or without your consent or help, so the worst comment you can make is, "No comment." It is better to be proactive and provide your own version of the story and have your "sound bite" reported. Without your comments, a reporter may have only the snippy words of a 13-year-old who says, "Yeah, we all got guns and we run this school."

2. Communicate consistent messages using a single designated spokesperson who is knowledgeable about the subject matter and has training in dealing with the media. Make sure the designated media spokesperson knows your media policy and procedures in advance. When dealing with school security issues, a professional security director or school police chief may have a greater effect on the media and still reflect a positive image for the district because that person is a credible source on the subject.

3. Explain systems, processes, and strategies, especially if you do not have details or if you are not ready to release details. For example, if a gang-related riot occurs at your school and 25 kids are taken to the police station at 7:45 A.M., you probably do not have enough facts for a media statement at 8:30 A.M. Explain that you are investigating the incident, taking statements, sharing information with law enforcement and that the results of your investigations will be aggressively pursued with disciplinary action, and when appropriate, prosecution. You have explained what you will

do, while at the same time not giving specific information or misinformation.

4. Try to be honest, responsive, and accessible, as hard as it may be. If you truly have absolutely nothing to say at the time you are contacted, tell the reporter when you will get back to him or her with a statement. Most important, keep your word and do so in a timely manner, to respect the reporter's deadline.

5. Get all of your side of the story out first. The best defense is a good offense.

6. Get to know the reporters, editors, and publishers who cover your education beat. Invite them for lunch twice a year for both sides to have a "gripe" session about the way your school and the media handle issues. Make sure your school security leader is involved because security issues so often make news stories.

7. Sell your positive efforts to the media. Invite them in as a part of the process, not to report on the process. If the media are represented in your school security planning process as community stakeholders, the story will eventually follow. And it will usually be in a positive, more favorable light than if they are called in as "outsiders."

Finally, anticipate the fact that somewhere in your educational career, especially if you are an administrator, you will face reporters. Also anticipate school security to be one of the issues you might have to address. You probably did not create the problem, but you must be able to deal with it. There is no reason why you should feel embarrassed or defensive in publicly explaining what happened if you took reasonable steps to prevent and/or manage it!

Where Do We Go From Here?

School security is growing out of its infancy as a profession. As the field quickly moves through the growing pains of puberty, many changes are likely to occur. Several items need to be on the agenda for the next developmental stage.

Legislation and Funding

At of this writing, a handful of states has legislation in the books regarding mandatory crime reporting and school security issues. Many of these were passed within the last 3 to 5 years. Unfortunately, the crime reporting issue has a long way to go before meeting an acceptable standard.

Crime reporting legislation, although well intentioned, has been incomplete, fragmented, and basically not enforced in most states. Most crime reporting legislation usually has no follow-up to ensure compliance and no "teeth" for those who fail to comply. Politically, most legislators prefer not to push the issue because of their fears of powerful education associations who lobby against it.

Those states that have passed mandatory crime reporting legislation have very different versions. The bottom line: little consistency nationally in crime reporting and data collection. The implications: poor databases and information sources for effective national policy and funding for school security and continued funding for intervention and prevention programs to be implemented in unsafe or unstable environments created, in part, by nonreporting. The need: national legislation mandating consistent crime reporting for elementary and secondary schools similar to that mandated of colleges and universities.

Funding sources should continue to include school security as a "fundable" priority item in their grant programs. It is time for educational systems to stop apologizing for enforcing the laws on school grounds. Security is a critical issue in providing safe environments conducive to effective education and prevention and intervention programming.

Improvements have been made in recent years to balance funding programs across the lines of prevention, intervention, and enforcement. Equally important is the growing number of requirements that funded projects must involve multiagency collaboration. Such balanced approaches and multiagency collaborations offer no guarantees, but they offer greater logic and hope for more effective programming.

Education and Training

School security has finally hit the agendas for professional conferences, seminars, workshops, and in-service training in recent years. Unfortunately, it usually hits the agenda after a crisis or high profile security-related incident. In fairness to educators, a growing number of sessions are being held from a prevention perspective, an applaudable act that school officials should be proud of, not apologetic!

School security needs to move one step further, however, on the educator's education agenda. Colleges and universities must begin incorporating mandatory classes on school security issues into teacher preparation courses, as well as into administrator and counseling certification programs. Graduate level classes and continuing education workshops on school security also should be regular, ongoing parts of the college agenda.

Beyond the Basics

Practical School Security looks at the myths, realities, processes, components, and strategies associated with basic professional school security. It is designed to give educators and members of the broader school community a handy basic reference and a no-nonsense look at school security from the perspective of a veteran school security official. Readers who are now aware that the issues touched on here are complex and require specialized education, training, and experience have learned the true lessons behind this book.

School security will likely see significant growth in future years as a profession. There must also be a coinciding growth in professional writing and professional development on the subject. *Practical School Security* represents a sincere contribution to professional school security and to the profession of school security.

References

American Association of School Administrators. (1981). *Reporting: Violence, vandalism and other incidents in schools.* Arlington, VA: Author.

American Society for Industrial Security. (1996). *Career opportunities in security.* Arlington, VA: Author.

Hill, M. S. & Hill, F. W. (1994). *Creating safe schools.* Thousand Oaks, CA: Corwin.

Huff, C. R. (1988, May). *Youth gangs and public policy in Ohio: Findings and recommendations.* Paper presented at the meeting of the Ohio Conference on Youth Gangs and the Urban Underclass, Columbus.

Kodluboy, D. W., & Evenrud, L. A. (1993). School-based interventions: Best practices and critical issues. In A. P. Goldstein & C. R. Huff (Eds.), *The gang intervention handbook* (pp. 257-294). Champaign, IL: Research Press.

Lal, S. R., Lal, D., & Achilles, C. M. (1993). *Handbook on gangs in schools: Strategies to reduce gang-related activities* (pp. 7-8). Thousand Oaks, CA: Corwin.

Quarles, C. L. (1993). *Staying safe at school.* Thousand Oaks, CA: Corwin.

Rubel, R. J., & Ames, N. (1986). *Reducing school crime and student misbehavior: A problem-solving strategy.* Rockville, MD: National Institute of Justice.

Spergel, I. A. (1990). Youth gangs: Continuity and change. In M. Tonry & N. Morris (Eds.), *Crime and justice: A review of research* (Vol. 12). Chicago: University of Chicago Press.

Taylor, C. S. (1988). Youth gangs organize quest for power, money. In *School Safety: National School Safety Center News Journal* (pp. 26-27). Malibu, CA: Pepperdine University Press.

Trump, K. S. (1996). Gang development and strategies in schools and suburban communities. In C. R. Huff (Ed.), *Gangs in America* (2nd ed., pp. 270-280). Thousand Oaks, CA: Sage.

Trump, K. S. (1997a). [School Crime Survey]. Unpublished raw data.

NATIONAL UNIVERSITY LIBRARY ORANGE COUNTY

Trump, K. S. (1997b). Security policy, personnel, and operations. In J. Conoley & A. Goldstein (Ed.), *The school violence intervention handbook,* (pp. 265-289). New York: Guilford.

U.S. Congress, Office of Technology Assessment. (1995). *Risks to students in school* (OTA Publication No. ENV-633). Washington, DC: Government Printing Office.

U.S. Department of Health, Education, and Welfare. (1978). *Violent schools—Safe schools: The safe school study report to Congress* (Vol. 1, p. 75). Washington, DC: Government Printing Office.

Recommended Readings

Conoley, J., & Goldstein, A. (1997). *The school violence intervention handbook*. New York: Guilford.

Hoffman, A. M. (1996). *Schools, violence, and society*. New York: Praeger.

Hoover, S., & Achilles, C. M. (1996). *Let's make a deal: Collaborating on a full-service school with your community*. Thousand Oaks, CA: Corwin.

Huff, C. R. (1996). *Gangs in America* (2nd ed.). Thousand Oaks, CA: Sage.

Hylton, J. B. (1996). *Safe schools: A security and loss prevention plan*. Newton, MA: Butterworth-Heinemann.

Lal, S. R., Lal, D., & Achilles, C. M. (1993). *Handbook on gangs in schools: Strategies to reduce gang-related activities*. Thousand Oaks, CA: Corwin.